HOOKER'S POLITY
IN MODERN ENGLISH

THE ECCLESIASTICAL POLITY ABRIDGED AND PARAPHRASED

JOHN S. MARSHALL
Professor of Philosophy
The University of the South

WIPF & STOCK · Eugene, Oregon

Wipf and Stock Publishers
199 W 8th Ave, Suite 3
Eugene, OR 97401

Hooker's Polity in Modern English
The Ecclesiastical Polity, Abidged and Paraphrased
By Marshall, John S. and Hooker, Richard
Softcover ISBN-13: 978-1-7252-7137-1
Publication date 3/2/2020
Previously published by University of the South, 1948

This work was assisted by a grant made conjointly by the Carnegie Foundation for the Advancement of Teaching and The University of the South. To both the Foundation and the University I express my sincere thanks.

PREFACE

THE name of Hooker is familiar to the educated man, but his monumental work on *Ecclesiastical Polity* is honored more by reputation than by careful reading. The average reader only knows his name, and even the well-informed theologian or political scientist seldom has more information about him than can be found in the textbooks and encyclopaedias. Even scholars know him only by reputation and have no accurate knowledge of his system of thought.

It is true the rare student who has mastered Hooker recognizes his greatness, but he cannot persuade others to consider a system of thought which in many respects is unique in the history of the English-speaking world. F. C. S. Northrop considers Hooker the fundamental thinker of all modern English civilization; D'Entreves places him in the highest rank of political thinkers, the one who has carried over the best of mediaeval thought into the modern world. Yet Hooker is not read.

The reason for this neglect is not far to seek. The *Ecclesiastical Polity* is really a work of controversy; it is a very elaborate answer to Thomas Cartwright's attacks upon the Anglican communion, an answer in which Cartwright's writings are answered by chapter and verse. Cartwright's arguments are now forgotten, and his works are unobtainable, and so much that Hooker has written has lost its meaning for the modern reader, unfamiliar as he is with these forgotten Elizabethan controversies.

The *Polity* is, of course, not only a refutation; it is an elaborate constructive argument as well. More than that, it is a justification and explanation of a certain conception of the Church, of the state, and of Christian civilization. All of these threads are woven into the designs of a single tapestry, for Hooker is not only a philosopher, a theologian, a political theorist, a controversialist, he is also a literary artist of high merit and gifts, and his methods of literary organization make possible this weaving of many strands into one fabric.

His literary style is recognized by such critics as Saintsbury, but his powers of literary organization are not so well known. He writes his master work as Sir Philip Sidney did his *Arcadia*, and as William Shakespeare did his *As You Like It*. The artistic method is similar to that of polyphonic music. In polyphony there are several melodies that are harmonized together to form the total composition; in the *Polity* there are several interlocking arguments that make up the one argument in its many complex phases.

Such a work is intelligible in its entirety only to the reader who hears every distinct melody within the highly complex harmony of the whole. Some of the melodic elements, however, are not intelligible to us today, and more than that, such polyphonic philosophical and theological writings are alien to our thought. What we need is a transposition of Hooker's argument into a modern form. I have rewritten Hooker much as a modern musician transposes a harpsichord composition of Bach for use on the modern piano; I have written out a simple melody, and then harmonized other factors with it. The melody becomes prominent, and other factors are subordinated.

What we have, therefore, in this paraphrase, is Hooker's argument stated as a system founded on a theory of law, and developed into a theory of redemption through the theory of the incarnation. The Church and the sacraments are instruments of the restoration of that fulness of life which is a participation in the life of God. The Church and the state are also revealed as agents of God's redemptive action in the world. The argument is clear and relatively simple, and is given in this paraphrase as a system of thought developing before the eyes of the reader from foundation to superstructure.

Much, however, is lost in such a selective process; the rich complexity of the tapestry or the polyphony disappears. The artistry of the Tudor writer gives place to the simplicity of the theological philosopher. In such a rewriting the method is vastly more Aristotelian than it is in Hooker's own book. What we have done is to select those passages that are relatively free from controversy and which develop from beginning to end a positive linear development from the foundations to the superstructure of his system.

The method gives us a clear and simple outline of the positive elements of his thought system, but lacks the variety which is really a part of Hooker's thought. Thus, we miss his clever criticism of contemporary thought, his refutation of Roman Catholic and Lutheran theology, his critique of contemporary political systems. All of this is sacrificed to an exposition of the positive and systematic elements of his thought.

The gain, however, is significant. The average reader can readily learn what Hooker has to say about the theory of law in relation to the universe, the Church, and the state. He discovers that Hooker is attempting to defend constitutional government against both absolutism and religious anarchy. He learns that Christian theology is set in the framework of an orderly universe and is not sharply separated from philosophy and science. He finds out that Hooker dislikes revolutionary democracy as much as he does lawless absolutism. What Hooker, therefore, defends is constitutional rule governed by law, and administered by a law-abiding sovereign who defends liberty as the law of Christianity. Such a constitutional Christian state is the hope of civilization.

As the language in which Hooker wrote was both complex and elyptical it has seemed wise to restate his words in modern idiom, and to expand his sentences in order to make the implications of his argument explicit. Thus, by a process of transposing a Tudor literary work of controversy into a book expressing a direct and positive argument, and by the restatement of Hooker's sentences in modern form, we have produced a work which declares an essentially modern argument in essentially modern idiom. So Hooker speaks once more in modern words a message to the modern man, for it is a modern message and is as relevant today as it was in the reign of Queen Elizabeth.

The argument is simple enough when it is freed from the controversies of the days in which Hooker lived. It is an exposition of the meaning of law both in the universe and in human society. It is a declaration of the failure of man and his restoration without the destruction of law. According to Hooker, the order of the world is divine and has its source in God. God is not only the Creator of the world, but he is the source of law.

Therefore, the world and all that therein is, and the heaven of heavens, form one kingdom over which God rules as Lord. God's kingdom has many levels, and man only finds his complete happiness by participating in every level of reality including the life of God himself. Man's disobedience and fall have alienated him from God and have destroyed that allegiance that bound the human creature to God as King. No longer are men the loving subjects of the Kingdom of Heaven, but rebellious aliens under God's coercive rule.

To restore these rebellious aliens to their place as loving subjects of his Kingdom, God sent down to men his Son who was both God and Man, and through the mediatorship of Jesus Christ the participation of men in the life of the Kingdom has been made possible once more. The Church, the ministry, and the sacraments are instruments of this restoration, instruments of the high priestly work of the ascended Christ. However, the priestly work is not all of Christ's work, for he is not only the great High Priest, he is King of Kings as well, and through his kingly rule there is a lordship over states which results not only in bliss for the world to come, but a better temporal order for this world.

Here is a philosophical theology in which God is Lord and King, in which his rule is law and order, in which the Bible is the word of God and Jesus Christ the Savior of men, in which the Church and the sacraments are means of participation in Christ, in which the Church and the ministry are divine institutions, in which the kingship of Jesus Christ is the hope of this world as well as the world to come.

This paraphrase is based on Keble's text of Richard Hooker, *Of the Laws of Ecclesiastical Polity*, arranged by John Keble, 7th ed., revised by R. W. Church and F. Paget, Oxford: Clarendon Press, 1888. The debt of any student of Hooker to John Keble's monumental work is enormous, but I have also found two other books of great assistance, Ronald Bayne's *Of the Laws of Ecclesiastical Polity, the Fifth Book*, London: Macmillan, 1902, and F. Paget's *Introduction to the Fifth Book of Hooker's Ecclesiastical Polity*, Oxford: Clarendon Press, 1899. Bayne's notes on particular points are a treasury of information, and Paget's synopses of the general argument are equally valuable. However, Bayne sometimes misses the meaning of a passage because he does not understand Hooker's general philosophy, and, therefore, needs correction; in this respect Paget is much his superior. As Paget does not interpret individual passages the two writers supplement each other in the interpretation of the Fifth Book.

Hooker used the Geneva Bible and almost invariably quoted from it. To make the paraphrase more usable to the modern reader I have changed the passages cited from the Geneva Version to the Authorized Version of 1611. Where Hooker has made his own translations from classical authors or from the

Fathers, I have modernized Hooker's English; and have used either the indication of sources made by Keble, or that made by Bayne where he has pointed out that the Migne text is approximately that used by Hooker.

In this labor of enthusiasm and love I have been particularly inspired by two of my fellow-faculty members, Professor T. S. Long, Chairman of the Department of English, and the Rev. Robert Manning, Assistant Chaplain. The three of us have read Hooker together to our mutual benefit and advantage.

For criticism of the diction and punctuation I have to thank Mr. Harold Barrett and Mr. Dwaine Filkins, faithful friends and loyal students.

J. S. M.

CONTENTS

PREFACE - v

PART ONE
GOD AND THE LAW

CHAPTER
- I. THE NECESSITY OF LAW - - - - - - - - - - 1
    Eccl. Pol., I.i.1., 2., 3 (part).
- II. GOD AND ETERNAL LAW - - - - - - - - - - 4
    Eccl. Pol., I.i. 3 (end)., ii. 1-6., iii.1.
- III. THE NATURAL LAW - - - - - - - - - - - - 11
    Eccl. Pol., I. iii. 2-5.
- IV. THE LAW FOR VOLUNTARY AGENTS - - - - - - - 18
    Eccl. Pol., I.v. 1-3., vii. 1-2., 3 (part)., viii. 1.
- V. THE LAW OF REASON - - - - - - - - - - - - 23
    Eccl. Pol., I. viii. 4., 8-9., ix. 1-2.
- VI. HUMAN LAWS AND THE BODY POLITIC - - - - - - 30
    Eccl. Pol., I. x. 1., 5-8
- VII. SUPERNATURAL LAW AND HUMAN FELICITY - - - - 36
    Eccl. Pol., I. xi. 1-5 (selections).

PART TWO
THE INCARNATION AND THE SACRAMENTS

CHAPTER
- VIII. THE SCRIPTURES AND THE WAY OF SALVATION - - - 45
    Eccl. Pol., I. xi. 6., xiv. 3-4., 5 (part)., xv. 4 (part).
- IX. PRAYER AND SACRAMENT - - - - - - - - - - 51
    Eccl. Pol., V. xxiii. 1., xlviii. 3 (part)., xlix. 4-5., l. 1-3.
- X. THE PERSONAL INCARNATION OF THE SON OF GOD - - 57
    Eccl. Pol., V. li. 1-3., lii. 3 (part)., 4 (part).
- XI. THE UNION OF THE TWO NATURES OF CHRIST - - - 62
    Eccl. Pol., V. liii. 3., 4 (part)., liv. 1-4., 6-8.
- XII. THE OMNIPRESENCE OF CHRIST - - - - - - - - 68
    Eccl. Pol., V. lv. 1-3., 6., 7 (part)., 8-9.
- XIII. PARTICIPATION IN CHRIST - - - - - - - - - 74
    Eccl. Pol., V. lvi. 1., 2 (part)., 3-4., 5 (parts)., 6., 7 (part)., 8., 10 (parts)., 13.

XIV. THE NECESSITY OF THE SACRAMENTS FOR PARTICIPATION IN CHRIST - - - - - - - - - - - - - - - 80
Eccl. Pol., V. lvii. 1-6.

XV. THE SACRAMENT OF BAPTISM - - - - - - - - - 85
Eccl. Pol., V. lviii. 1-4., lx. 1-2.

XVI. THE SACRAMENT OF THE BODY AND BLOOD OF CHRIST - 89
Eccl. Pol., V. lxvii. 1-2., 4-7.

PART THREE

THE ORDERS OF THE MINISTRY

CHAPTER

XVII. THE CHURCH MYSTICAL AND THE CHURCH VISIBLE - - 97
Eccl. Pol., III. i. 2-8.

XVIII. THE CHURCH, THE MINISTRY, AND TEMPORAL HAPPINESS 104
Eccl. Pol., V. lxxvi. 1 (part)., 2 (part)., 3., 4 (part)., 5., 9-10.

XIX. THE MINISTRY OF THINGS DIVINE - - - - - - - 110
Eccl. Pol., V. lxxvii. 1-2., 5-8 (selections).

XX. THE THREE DEGREES OF ECCLESIASTICAL ORDER IN THE MINISTRY - - - - - - - - - - - - - - - - 116
Eccl. Pol., V. lxxviii. 2 (part)., 3-4., 5 (parts).

XXI. BISHOPS IN THE CHURCH OF CHRIST - - - - - - 121
Eccl. Pol., VII. iv. 1., 3-4., vi. 1., 3., 8 (parts).

PART FOUR

CHURCH AND STATE

CHAPTER

XXII. CHURCH AND STATE AS ONE - - - - - - - - - 127
Eccl. Pol., VIII. i. 2 (part)., 4 (part)., 5 (part).

XXIII. THE KING AS A LIMITED SOVEREIGN - - - - - - 132
Eccl. Pol., VIII. ii. 1 (part)., 2., 5 (parts)., 6., 11., 12 (part)., 13.

XXIV. THE KING AS TEMPORAL HEAD OF THE CHURCH - - - 137
Eccl. Pol., VIII. iii. 2 (part)., 3., iv. 1., 2 (part)., 5.

XXV. CHRIST AS SUPREME SOVEREIGN - - - - - - - - 141
Eccl. Pol., VIII. iv. 6 (parts).

XXVI. CHRIST AS SPIRITUAL HEAD OF THE CHURCH - - - - 147
Eccl. Pol., VIII. iv. 7 (parts)., 10 (part)., 12.

PART ONE

GOD AND THE LAW

Chapter I. The Necessity of Law
Chapter II. God and Eternal Law
Chapter III. The Natural Law
Chapter IV. The Law for Voluntary Agents
Chapter V. The Law of Reason
Chapter VI. Human Laws and the Body Politic
Chapter VII. Supernatural Law and Human Felicity

CHAPTER I

THE NECESSITY OF LAW

IF a man sets out to persuade the masses that they are not as well governed as they ought to be, he will never lack attentive and favorably disposed hearers, because the masses know the many defects to be found in every kind of government. However, these same people do not ordinarily have the insight to consider the hidden hindrances and numerous difficulties inevitable in public affairs. Those who openly condemn the supposed disorders of the state seem to be preeminently interested in the general well-being of everyone, and unusually open-minded as well. Because of their good reputation, whatever they say seems to be good and genuine. That which is lacking in their persuasive power is supplied by the tendency of their hearers to accept and believe them.

However, we who favor the established order of things have to face two difficulties. First, we must combat a number of intense prejudices deeply rooted in the minds of those who think that we are timeservers, favorable to the existing state of things either because we already have preferment or else because we seek it. Second, we must bear with the objections usually brought against arguments by persons as prejudiced as our opponents are against that which they do not wish to have thrust upon them.

Therefore, much of what we say may seem to some people tedious, obscure, and intricate. We know this to be so because many people talk about the truth who have never plumbed the depths from which it comes; and so when we try to lead them to those depths they soon grow weary, like men led away from the beaten paths to which they have been accustomed. Despite the tediousness which they suffer, the opposition of such men is not strong enough to prevent our exposition of what is appropriate to the truth, and we will proceed whether the delicate mood of certain people is pleased with our exposition or not.

Those who find us tedious are not injured by us, because they can always spare themselves the pain of reading our work if they wish. If anybody complains about our obscurity he must remember that the matters treated by us are very much like many of the works of art and nature, where that which is of the most importance is not visible in what we see. The grandeur of houses, the beauty of trees delight us when we see them. But the foundation which supports the house, and the root which nourishes and gives life to the tree, are hidden in the bowels of the earth. If at any time we want to find the foundation of the house or the root of the tree we shall discover that the labor involved is more a hard necessity than a pleasure, and that is true not only for those who do the work but even for those who watch those who labor.

What is true of houses and trees is true of good laws as well, for all those who live under the laws enjoy the pleasure and comfort of them even though they do not know the foundation and original root from which they grow. As a matter of fact, most men have no knowledge of these roots, and all is well so long as they obey the laws and enjoy the comfort of them, even though they do not know the roots from which they have grown. However, when human beings disobey the laws and then pretend that those very laws which they should obey are corrupt and vicious, then we must uncover the foundations that underlie our legal system. If we are to examine the quality of our laws, we must lay bare the very foundation and root, the deepest source of the law. And because we do not often put ourselves to the trouble of digging down to these foundations, when we do so, we find that the trouble we must take, even though necessary, is not very pleasant. We are not accustomed to seek out the foundations of the laws, and hence, because of their very novelty, they seem obscure, intricate, and unfamiliar, until the mind grows better acquainted with them.

I wish to make the task as simple as possible for the reader, and so throughout the whole argument I have tried to make the earlier parts the basis of that which follows later in the book, and the latter parts a source of illumination of the earlier parts. If those who read the book will only wait and learn the meaning of the more general principles they will see their meaning applied in the latter part of the book, and much that seems obscure at first will be found to be much clearer in the later pages of the book. Also the particular points made in the latter portion of the book will appear better grounded if their foundations have been discerned in the earlier part of the book.

The laws of the Church have been called in question. From times long past we have been guided by them in the exercise of the Christian Religion and of the service of the only true God. They are our rites, our customs, and the orders of ecclesiastical government. These ancient laws are called in question by men who accuse us and say that we refuse to have Jesus Christ rule over us. They say that we have wilfully cast his laws behind our backs because we dislike to be reformed and because we do not wish to submit ourselves to his rule and discipline. It is because of this charge that we present for a general trial at the hands of the whole world those laws of the Church under which we live.

As we do this, we heartily beseech Almighty God, whom we desire to serve according to his will, that he will cause us completely to lay aside all prejudice and partiality, and we pray him that we may have eyes to see and hearts to embrace the things that are most acceptable in his sight.

CHAPTER II

God and Eternal Law

THE point about which there is a difference of opinion is the nature of our laws, and so we cannot deal with this problem better than by considering first the nature of law in general, and, second, the nature of the law according to which the Eternal himself does his work, that law which gives significance to all other laws. Next, we shall proceed to a consideration of the law, first of nature, then of Scripture. In this way we shall have an easier access to the things which we shall consider later.

Everything that exists has an operation or particular form of activity that is not constrained or accidental, and nothing begins to function according to this operation without some planned purpose toward which it works. The purpose cannot be realized unless the work done is suited to the purpose of obtaining it, for every purpose cannot be realized by every kind of operation. A law is that which assigns to each thing its type or kind, which moderates the force and power of the thing, and which appoints the form and measure of its activity. Therefore, no definite purpose could be realized unless the actions by which it is realized were orderly. This means that they would have to be suitable and fit, and that they should correspond by some canon, rule, or law, to the end which they are to achieve. Even in the activities of God himself, which are the source of all other activities, there is this correspondence and this law. Everything, therefore, functions to some extent according to law. Some things operate according to a law, the author of which is superior to them, and to whom they are subject.

All other things are the works and operations of God himself, and in this case God is the worker and the source of the law according to which they are wrought. The being of God is a kind of law to his working, for the perfection of God gives perfection to everything he does. Those natural, necessary, and internal activities of God, namely the generation of the Son, and the procession of the Spirit, are outside of the limits of the present discussion. Our business is only with those activities which have their beginning and their very existence solely through voluntary purpose, a purpose through which God has decreed when and how such activities should be. This eternal decree is what we call an eternal law.

It would be dangerous for the feeble brain of man to penetrate too far into the doings of the Most-High, for it is life to know him, and joy to make mention of his name, but our soundest knowledge is to know that we do not know him as he really is, and to know that we cannot know him. Our safest eloquence concerning him is our silence, when we confess without confession that his glory is inexplicable and that his greatness is above our capacity and reach. He is above and we are on earth; and therefore it befits us that our words be cautious and that they be few.[1]

Our God is one. He is very *Oneness*, and mere unity. The unity of God is nothing but itself in itself, and does not consist, as all other things beside God do, of many things. Even so, a personal Trinity subsists in this essential unity of God, after a manner that far transcends man's understanding. The external acts of God are of such a kind that they proceed from him as a unity, and yet each person of the Trinity contributes to them something peculiar and restricted to itself. For although they are three, the members of the Trinity all subsist in the essence of one Deity, and from the Father, by the Son, through the Spirit, all things exist. That which the Son hears of the Father, and is then received by the Spirit from the Father and the Son, the same we receive from the Spirit as

[1] Eccl. 5. 2.

being the third in order; and therefore the nearest to us, although, we must add, the power of the Spirit is that of the Second and the First.[2]

Even the wise and learned men among the very heathens themselves have acknowledged that there was some first cause upon which all things depend. Likewise, they never spoke of that cause in any other terms than as an agent who knew what and why he worked and who observed in his working a most exact order or law. They all confess that in the working of that first cause a plan is used, a reason is followed, a way observed. That means that constant order and law are observed, and that the First Cause must of necessity be the author of that very order and law which it itself obeys.

If this were not so, and there were some author of the order and law above the First Cause, then the First Cause would not be a first Cause. However, since it is the First Cause, there can be no other author besides itself of that order and law according to which it willingly works. God, therefore, is a law both to himself and to all other things besides. He is a law to himself in all those things spoken of by our Savior when he says, "My Father worketh hitherto, and I work."[3]

God does not work without a reason. Everything he does has some purpose for which it is done, and the purpose for which it is done is the reason why he wills to do it. He would never have wished to create woman unless he had seen that it would not be well if she were not created. "It is not good that the man should be alone; I will make him an help meet for him."[4] God only does that which would not be good if it were left undone, and he does nothing else.

If we ask why it is that, although God has infinite power and capacity, the results wrought by that power are all as limited as we see them to be, the answer is that the purpose which he

[2] Jn. 16. 13-15.
[3] Jn. 5. 17.
[4] Gen. 2. 18.

sets before himself and the law he uses have modified the effects of his power in such a way that the power does not work infinitely, but is fitted to the purpose that it is trying to achieve. And thus all things are created in most decent and comely sort, all things in "Measure, and Number, and Weight."[5]

The general purpose of God's operations outside of himself is the exercise of his most glorious and most abundant virtue. This abundance is manifest in variety and for this reason is oftentimes called *riches* in the Scriptures.[6] "The Lord hath made all things for himself."[7] That does not mean that anything is created for his good but all things are created so that he can reveal his goodness and kindness through them. On the other hand the particular end of every act that proceeds from God as an external act is not possible to be understood. Hence, we cannot always give the particular and absolutely certain reason for what he does. However, there is undoubtedly a unique and absolutely certain reason for every finite work of God, and we know that because there is a law imposed upon it. If there were no such law imposed upon it, the finite work would be infinite, even as God, the worker himself, is.

Those persons are mistaken who think that when God wills to do this or that he has no reason for doing so besides the fact that he wishes to do so. Often we know no reason why God has willed to do what he has, but that there is no reason beside that of his mere will, I think it would be most unreasonable to imagine; because he "worketh all things after the counsel of his own will"[8] and not merely according to his own will. Whatever is done with counsel or wise planning necessarily has some reason why it should be done, although the reason may be often so hidden from us that it forces the intelligence of man to stand amazed at it. The Apostle was himself amazed, and said, "O

[5] Wis. 11. 20.
[6] Eph. 3. 16.
[7] Prov. 16. 4.
[8] Eph. 1. 11.

the depth of the riches both of the wisdom and knowledge of God! how unsearchable are his judgments, and his ways past finding out!"[9]

There is an eternal law which God has created for himself, and in accordance with this law he makes all things of which he is the cause and author. That law is the admirable framework in which the perfect beauty of the wisdom of God reveals her face. Wisdom says of herself, "The Lord possessed me in the beginning of his way, before his works of old."[10] The eternal law was the pattern for the making of the world, and the map for the guidance of the world. It has been with God and will be with God forever, and God is its only author and guardian. If this is so, how can either men or angels perfectly apprehend it? The book of this law we are neither able nor worthy to open and to look into. The little part of the law which we dimly comprehend we admire. The rest we humbly adore with religious ignorance. Therefore, God works according to his eternal law, "for of him, and through him, and to him, are all things."[11] Even though the affairs of this present world seem to us to be in confusion and disorder, "let no one doubt but that everything is done well because the world is ruled by so good a guide."[12] He is a good guide because he does not transgress his own law, a law which is the most absolute, perfect, and just.

The law according to which God works is eternal, and therefore has no manifestation or even semblance of change. Hence, a part of that law has been manifest in the promises which God has made. That is because his promises are nothing else except what God will do for the good of men. When the Apostle speaks of these promises he tells us that God could as readily "deny himself"[13] and not be God, as to fail to fulfill his prom-

[9] Rom. 11. 33.
[10] Prov. 8. 22.
[11] Rom. 11. 36.
[12] Boeth., *de consol.*, bk. iv.
[13] 2 Tim. 2. 13.

ises. And when the Apostle speaks of the counsel of God he also calls it a thing "unchangeable."[14] The counsel of God and the law of God are one and the same.

God's freedom of will is not to any degree reduced or limited by this eternal law because the imposition of this law upon himself is God's own free and voluntary act. This law we may, therefore, call eternal because it is that order which God before all ages has assigned to himself as the rule according to which he will do all things.

I am not ignorant of the fact that when the learned use the expression *the law eternal* they do not mean that order which God has eternally planned to be observed in all his works, but they mean that rule which he has determined as one expedient to be kept by all his creatures in accordance with the several characteristics with which he has endowed them. Those who use the word law in this way mean by it a rule of action which must be imposed by a superior authority. But we give a wider meaning to the term, and use the term law for any rule according to which actions are given shape. Now the law for all creatures, which they call eternal because it is laid up in the bosom of God, we also call eternal; but, because it is the rule of things, we call it the second law eternal, whereas the law of God's own action is called the first law eternal.

This second law eternal has different kinds of names depending upon the different kinds of things which are subject to it. That part of the second law eternal which gives order to natural agents we usually call nature's law. That part of the law which angels clearly behold and obey without deviation is the celestial and heavenly law. That part is called the law of reason which legally constrains the reasonable creatures of this world, and it is a law which reasonable creatures may most clearly perceive, by reason, as constraining them. That part of

[14]Heb. 6. 17. (Revised Standard Version).

the law which binds them but is not known except by a special revelation of God is called divine law.

Human law is that law which men think to be expedient and make into a law, using either the law of reason or of God as a clue to their action. Everything, therefore, which is as it ought to be, conforms to the second law eternal. Even those things which do not conform to the second eternal law do have some order imposed upon them by the first eternal law. For whatever exists under the sun, whether it be good or evil, and whatever action there is, whether it corresponds to the law which God has imposed upon his creatures or whether it is incompatible with that law, God works upon it in accordance with the law which he has determined from eternity to use. That means that all things whether good or evil are under the first law eternal. Thus, there is a two-fold law eternal which God has created, and it is not difficult to see that they both operate in **everything that exists.**

CHAPTER III

The Natural Law

WE now begin our treatment of the law of nature. We sometimes mean by the law of nature the manner of operation that God has set for each and every thing that he has created. However, we should more accurately term those agents natural agents which unconsciously observe the law of their type. Such natural agents are the heavens and the elements of the world. These can act in no other way than the way they do. Hence, their law of operation more appropriately is called natural law.

Intelligent beings we do not usually call natural agents, but we term them voluntary agents, a term we use to distinguish them from the agents that act unconsciously. Now, since these two are different, it is useful to distinguish the unconscious from the voluntary agents. The unconscious agents, which we have called natural agents, adhere to the law of their nature strictly. This is acknowledged by everyone. However, this law of involuntary agents involves more than men have yet understood or perhaps will ever understand, since God has made it difficult for the sons of man to understand it, for we know how much more complex the smallest thing is than the wisest man realizes. This should lead us to humility.

When Moses describes the work of creation he places words in the mouth of God. God said, "Let there be light: let there be a firmament: let the waters under the heaven be gathered together unto one place: let the earth bring forth: let there be lights in the firmament of heaven."[1] Did Moses mean to tell us that God's power revealed an infinite greatness because he produced such results so easily without labor, without difficulty,

[1] Gen. 1. 3-14.

without effort? Surely it seems that Moses means something more than this; he means that God did not work by sheer necessity, but rather as a voluntary agent who planned things beforehand and then decreed what he would produce external to himself. In the second place, Moses wants us to know that God instituted a natural law that was to be observed by the beings created by him.

Hence, we realize that these laws were established by a solemn injunction, just as all the laws of God were instituted. God commanded those things to be which now are; he commanded them to continue to act as they now do. This existence, this kind, this form of action, are therefore the same as the establishment of the law of nature. What is the first creation of this world, and the preservation since of the things that God created, but a manifestation in action of the eternal law of God for the natural world? It is just the same in the created world as it is in a human kingdom; for in a kingdom, after a law is once promulgated, it soon goes into operation far and wide, and all the regions under that king conform to that law. We ought to think that the natural course of the world is of a similar sort.

Since that day on which God first proclaimed the edicts of his law for the world, both heaven and earth have obeyed his command and their work has been to do his will. "He made a decree for the rain."[2] He "placed the sand for the bound of the sea by a perpetual decree, that it cannot pass it."[3] Suppose nature should interrupt her ordered manner of operation and even for a moment should cease to observe her own laws. Suppose the basic and primordial elements of the world, of which all things in this lower world are made, should lose the qualities which they now possess. Suppose the structure of that heavenly arch over our heads should disintegrate and dissolve. Suppose the celestial spheres should forget their usual motions,

[2] Job. 28. 26.
[3] Jer. 5. 22.

and should turn themselves in irregular motions in any accidental way that might happen. Suppose the prince of the lights of heaven who "rejoiceth as a giant to run his course"[4] should begin to stand still because he languished and was faint, and suppose he should rest himself. Suppose the moon should deviate from her beaten path, and the times of the seasons of the year should be disordered and confused, the winds breathe out their last breath, the clouds yield no rain; the earth, then, would have no dews from heaven, and the fruits and vegetables would shrivel up like children at the withered breast of a mother who could no longer feed them. Suppose all these irregularities and deviations from the law of nature should occur. What would become of man, who is served by all of them? Do we not see plainly that the obedience of all things created by God to the law of nature is the support of the world?

Despite this obedience and constancy of nature, the same thing sometimes happens to it as to art. Phidias did have the highest skill, it is true, but with refractory material for his carving, even his work would have lacked that beauty it would have had if the material had been better suited to the purpose. If the strings of a musical instrument are incapable of harmony even the skillful touch of the musician will produce only an unpleasant sound. Theophrastus tells us of that kind of matter to be found in many natural objects of such a character that much of it will not receive the best and most perfect impression. This defect in the material of natural things was observed by those ancient philosophers who studied nature; but they did not understand the real cause of the defect. Because of man's sin, God laid a divine curse on those of his creations which he made for human use.

But this conception was an article of that saving truth which God had revealed to his Church; hence, revelation was beyond the reach of the merely natural possibility of understanding of

[4]Ps. 19. 5. (Prayer Bk. Vers.)

the philosophers who came before the time of Christianity. Despite the deviations that are now and again incidental to the course of nature, the laws of nature are kept with such constancy by natural agents that no one denies that nature's operations are always or nearly always carried out in a uniform manner.

If at this point we are asked what it is that keeps nature obedient to its own law, we must refer to that higher, first eternal law, of which we have already spoken. That means that the law of nature as one part of the second eternal law depends on the first eternal law. Because all other law depends on the first eternal law we must explain the constancy of the law of nature by reference to the first eternal law. We do not believe, however, as some do, that nature as she works has before her certain models or patterns which subsist in the mind of the Highest, and are discovered there by her. We do not believe that nature keeps her eye fixed on these eternal models like travelers at sea who guide themselves by the polar star. We do not hold, therefore, that nature works out her designs by an imitation of the models in God's mind. Rather, we accept Hippocrates' position that "everything in all that it does fulfills the work which destiny has ordained." We also accept his conception of the way in which this is carried out, "for the things do not know what they do, and yet they operate as if they did know what they do, and as a matter of fact they do not see the thing at which they look."[5]

However, the works of nature are as accurate as if she did see some absolute shape or image before her, and as if she did try to imitate it. Indeed, her dexterity and her skill are such that no intellectual creature in the world has the ability to do what nature does without intellectual capacity and knowledge. This being so, nature must have some director whose infinite knowledge guides her in everything she does. But who is the

[5]Hp., pp. 342, 348. ed. Genev. 1657.

guide of nature unless it is the God of nature? "In him we live, and move, and have our being."⁶ The things which nature is said to do are worked out by God by the use of nature as an instrument. And nature has not in herself the divine knowledge requisite for her operations, but the knowledge is possessed by God, who is the guide of nature's work.

There are natural objects who are voluntary agents, but there are natural objects which are not voluntary agents, and it is only these with which we are dealing. These things, without volition, keep their fixed laws with such strict necessity that they cannot possibly do, or even tend to do, what they accomplish in any other manner than that which is their continual mode of operation. Of course, if through some external force their form is changed, then their form of operation changes as well. The kinds of activities are always precisely suited to the exact end for which the thing is fitted; but, although these natural things do what is appropriate, they do not know why they do it or what they do. Hence, everything they do that is in accordance with their purpose has its origin in an agent who knows, appoints, sustains, and even actually shapes them.

The way in which God does this transcends our understanding. We are no more able to understand it by our reason than the unreasoning creatures can understand by their senses how we arrange and order the course of our affairs. We understand only this much, that the natural production and process of all things receive their order of operation from the fixed constancy of the divine understanding. It is the divine wisdom that sets for them their diverse forms of operation. This order of operation that has its source in this purity of God's own knowledge and will we rightly call Providence. Since the ancients thought that this order belonged to the things themselves rather than to God they called it destiny. The law which we see operating in natural things in its authentic and original form is as if written

⁶Acts 17. 28.

in the inner life of God himself. It is God's spirit which puts the law into operation, and he uses every particular natural thing, every merely natural agent, simply as an instrument. As an instrument it was created at the beginning, and as an instrument it has been used ever since the beginning to carry out God's will and pleasure. Nature, therefore, is nothing else except God's instrument. It is said that when Dionysius saw a sudden disturbance in the order of nature he cried out, "Either God has been handicapped and thwarted by a greater than himself, or if that is impossible, then he has now decided to dissolve the world, for the law of the universe seems to have ceased to be carried out, and without it the world cannot stand."

This Creator whose servant nature is, is in truth only one being; but the heathens thought that he was more than one. In the sky they gave him the name of Jupiter, in the air that of Juno, in the water that of Neptune, in the earth that of Vesta or Ceres. They called him Apollo in the sun, in the moon they called him Diana, and by Aeolus and various other names in the winds. As a matter of fact, they imagined that nature had as many guides as there were natural things in the world, and they honored them as beings who could work or stop working as men actually deserved to have them work. But we believe that there is only one guide for all natural agents, and he is both the creator and author who causes all things to function as the instruments of his purpose; and he alone is to be blessed, adored, and honored by all forever.

Up to this point we have dealt with natural agents considered as individual things functioning in isolation. Now we ought to deal briefly with another factor besides that law which directs them by appropriate means to their own perfection. There is another law besides that which directs them to their own perfection. It is concerned with individual things as social beings united into one body. This is a law which obligates each one of them to serve the good of others and to prefer the good of the whole to that which is exclusively their own good. We clearly see this happen when natural objects disregard their ordinary natural inclination. Then that which is heavy rises up of its own accord and forsakes the center of the earth which is its natural level. It then acts as if it heard itself commanded to surrender the good it wishes for itself and to relieve the present communal distress of nature.

CHAPTER IV

THE LAW FOR VOLUNTARY AGENTS

GOD is the only being who is everlastingly and actually what he should be, and who cannot be anything which he is not now. Everything else contains potentiality, and may be in the future what it is not in the present. Because all things besides God are incomplete and may become what they now are not, they all have desire or have an inclination to be something which they may be but as yet are not. When they attain that which they desire they will be more perfect than they now are. All these perfections which come from the attainment of desire are grouped together under the general name of goodness. And since there is nothing in the world that does not add to the perfection of something else, anything that exists is good.

Desire leads us even further, for it leads to nothing less than the participation in God himself. This is true because there is no goodness that can be desired which does not come from God as the supreme cause of all things. And as everything produced either contains something of the cause which produced it, or at least resembles the cause, then everything in the world may be said in some way or other to seek the highest, who is God himself. However, this search for the highest does not appear so much in any other creature as it does in man, because there are so many kinds of perfection which humans seek.

The first stage of goodness is that general perfection sought by everything. It is the desire to continue to exist. Everything that exists desires to be like God by continuing to live forever; and the things that cannot attain a personal immortality try to perpetuate themselves by propagating themselves and by continuing to live in their offspring. The second stage of goodness is to be found in another sort of likeness to God. Each thing desires always to excel in just those functions which belong particularly to its kind. It desires the unchangeable character of God, and it tries to imitate him by always doing what it does after one and the same manner. It tries to imitate the absolute precision of God by trying to be exact in every particular thing it does. That is the reason for the axioms in philosophy which indicate that nature always aims at that which cannot be bettered.

These two kinds of goodness which we have just mentioned are so closely united to the things themselves which desire them that we are hardly aware of the desire that causes the action when it takes place. There is, however, a third kind of goodness, where there is no desire unless the object is first known, or else desired only for the knowledge itself. It is by a knowledge of the truth and by an exercise of virtue that man alone of the creatures of this lower world desires the highest possible conformity with God. That this is so is a thing known not only to those who have been instructed by God through revelation, but also to those who never had such a revelation. What thing is more common with Plato than his constant attempt to excite men to love wisdom by demonstrating how much wisdom exalts the wise man above all other men? Plato points out that knowledge carries man up to the very heavens and makes him even like unto the gods—high, admirable, and divine. And Hermes Trismegistus, when he speaks of the virtues of a righteous soul, says, "Such spirits are never weary of praising and speaking well of all men, and of doing good to everyone both by word and deed. That is because they model themselves after the likeness of the father of spirits."[1]

We know, through reason, the things that are the objects of sense, and the things that are not. It is obvious how we know the things of sense, but it is our problem to learn how we come to a knowledge of those things beyond sense if we are to have a guide to action. Since nothing can move unless there is an

[1] Her. Tris., c. 10, 21.

end that acts as a provocation which produces motion, our question is how that divine part of the soul which the Apostle calls the "spirit of your mind"[2] ever moves into action unless it also has some excitation.

The purpose which is the aim of our activity is sometimes the very good which we think lies in the activity itself without any further goodness at all. Then the cause of our action is the mere desire of action, and no other good besides that of the action lies in our purpose. It has been said of certain unruly persons, "They thought that the very disturbance of established institutions was a sufficient reward for their effort."[3] At other times what we do is referred to as an end beyond the activity, and then if there were no desire for that which transcends the activity we would not act. That is true of those who gave alms to receive the praises of men.

Man is made in the likeness of his Maker, not only in the perfection of his nature, but also in the way he does things. That is the reason that whatever we do as men we do consciously and of free will. That is the reason we are not so constrained as natural agents are, for they must act as they do, but we can leave the things we do undone. Unless we are conscious of the object of our action, and like and desire it, we neither work for the good which lies in action itself, nor for the good which transcends it. The fact that we work for any such purpose means that we choose it, and prefer to work for it rather than not. There is no choice unless the thing we do could have been rejected and left undone. If fire burns up the stubble it does not choose to burn it, but it does so because its nature is such that it could not have done otherwise. To choose is to will one thing instead of another. To will is to shape our souls either to the possessing or to the doing of that which they discern to be good. Goodness is seen with the eye of the under-

[2] Eph. 4. 23.
[3] Sallust., cat. 21.

standing, and the light of that eye is reason. Hence, the two chief fountains of human action are knowledge and will. Will, when it has a purpose, is called choice. Moses says of knowledge, "I have set before you life and death, blessing and cursing."[4] And about the will he says also, "choose life."[5] And by that he means that we must choose the things that lead to life.

However, we must be particularly careful of one thing of no small importance, and that is how the will, taken strictly as will and therefore as dealing with a purpose which is desired, differs sharply from that lower natural desire which is called appetite. The thing desired by the appetite is anything we wish because the senses lead us to it. The thing desired by the will is that good for which reason leads us to seek. Emotions such as joy, grief, fear, and anger, are different kinds and forms of appetite. These emotions do not surge up within us when we think of something that is quite indifferent to us; but at other times they will surge up at the sight of certain things. It is not wholly within our control, therefore, whether we will be stirred by certain emotions or not. But the actions which proceed from the attitudes of our will are wholly within our power to be done or left undone. Finally, we may say that appetite is the will's solicitor, and will is the appetite's controller. For what we desire as the object of appetite is often rejected by the will. The only desire which is appropriately called will is that in which reason and understanding show us what is to be desired.

Let us now deal with the way in which we discover those rules according to which the will of man ought to be guided in gaining goodness through human action. Man, like every natural thing, necessarily and naturally desires the utmost good and greatest perfection of which nature has made him capable. Since our happiness is the object and achievement of our desire, we cannot choose but to wish and to desire it. The will inclines to

[4] Deut. 30. 19.
[5] Ibid.

everything that can be achieved by action which reason judges to be superior for us, and because it is better for us it is the more capable of producing our happiness.

If reason makes a mistake we fall into evil, and in this way we are deprived of that general perfection we seek. Therefore, since the knowledge of the difference between good and evil is necessary for the shaping of human action, we must now find out how we may obtain this knowledge. In this investigation we must not assume that there is one rule for the good and another for the evil, because if we know the straight we have a guide for discerning the crooked. This is true because the absence of the straightness in a body that should be straight is itself crookedness. Since goodness in action is like straightness in a body, we call action that is well done *the right*. The straight path is most acceptable to the traveller because by it he can most quickly come to his journey's end. So it is in action, for that which lies most directly between us and the end we desire is most appropriate for our use.

In that which is most appropriate for our use there is also rectitude and beauty, as there is in the other kind of thing delinquency and deformity. That which is good in the actions of men not only delights us as profitable but as lovable as well. That is the reason that the Greeks had a kind of divine insight when they gave the active perfection of men a name that expressed both beauty and goodness. They called it καλοκαγαθία because goodness in ordinary language is usually applied only to the beneficial, and they wished to indicate that it included beauty as well. When we use the word goodness in this book we mean both.

CHAPTER V

THE LAW OF REASON

IN the broadest sense a law is a rule that indicates how an activity should function to realize the goodness which it is to achieve. The rule of the divine activities external to God himself is the definite decree of God's own wisdom which he has set down for himself.

The rule of natural agents is one which they follow by simple necessity. It is a decree of God's wisdom which is known to God himself as the principle director of natural objects, but is not known to the agents which are directed by God to carry them out. The rule of natural agents, such as animals, who in part work of their own accord, is a judgment that rests on common sense knowledge and imagination, and deals with that goodness of objects which is revealed to the senses, and it is by this sensory goodness that they are moved.

The rule of spiritual or immaterial natures such as angels is their intuitive or intellectual judgment concerning the lovable beauty and high goodness of God as the being who, with unspeakable joy and delight, sets them to work. The rule of voluntary agents on earth is that judgment given by reason concerning the goodness of those things which voluntary agents are to do. And the judgments given by reason,—sometimes more general judgments, sometimes less general,—are a preparation for the definition of those particular actions which are good.

Therefore, the natural measure by which we can judge our actions is the judgment of reason, for it is reason which determines and sets down for us what it is good for us to do. Sometimes the judgment of reason is mandatory, and then it points out what we must do. Sometimes it is permissive, and then it tells us only what we may do. At other times it is advisory, and reveals to us what is suitable for us to do.

There is a mandatory judgment of reason when there is a simple question of doing that thing which is absolutely good, and not doing that which is absolutely evil. That was the situation Joseph faced when it was a question of yielding or not yielding to the passionate desire of his lascivious mistress.[1] If he had yielded, it would have been absolute evil; as he did not yield, it was absolute good.

There is a permissive judgment of reason when we cannot avoid some evil, and must choose one out of several possibilities, and this is the situation only when the case is so urgent that we cannot do otherwise but make a choice. That is the reason that Moses allowed the Jews to write a bill of divorcement to put their wives away. Because of their hardness of heart, Moses had to choose the lesser of two evils, and allow divorce rather than some greater evil.[2]

There is an advisory judgment of reason when there is a choice of many good things before us, but one of them is of the first rank of importance and is preeminent. That was the case of those who sold their possessions "and brought the money, and laid it at the apostles' feet,"[3] for they might have kept them and done so without sin. The same was true of the Apostle Paul's decision to support himself by his own labor,[4] for if he had allowed the Church to maintain him he would have committed no evil.

Since there is a wide extent of goodness from which we may choose, there is a certain latitude in it, and therefore even among good actions some are better than others. If this were not so, one man would not be better than another. In that case an act would be either absolutely good or absolutely evil. It would

[1] Gen. 39. 7 ff.
[2] Mk. 10. 2-9.
[3] Acts 4. 37.
[4] 2 Thess. 3. 8.

be like the case of one who shot his arrow at an invisible point on the target, and either hit it or else did not. Either the man would hit the center, which is goodness, or else fail to do it and be excluded from the number who are good. If all goodness were so absolute, there would be no degrees of well-doing except in the infrequency or the frequency of well-doing. But there is a certain breadth of goodness, for it is not like a simple point.

Since this is true, a law may be appropriately defined as that which reason so defines to be good that it must be done. Thus the law of reason is that which men by the exercise of natural reason have rightly found to be the rules that bind them all forever in their actions.

Even the voluntary acts of those who keep the laws of reason have the most vivid resemblance to the exact method of operation which nature necessarily observes in the orderly process of the whole world. Thus it is that the laws of reason have several characteristics by which they are known. First of all, as the works of nature are all useful, beautiful, and without excess or defect, so are human voluntary actions if they are formed according to the rule taught by the law of reason. Second, these laws of reason can be investigated by reason without the aid of supernatural and divine revelation. In the third place, they have always been known, because they could be so readily ascertained that the knowledge about them is a general possession. That is what Sophocles means when he says about some branch of the law, "It is no child born today or even yesterday, but it has been in existence no one knows for how long."[5]

The law of reason is accepted not only by one or two or a few, but by everybody. This does not mean that every single person in the whole world knows the content of the law of reason and asserts it. It means, however, that when it is once presented to him no man can reject it as unreasonable and unjust.

[5] Soph., Antig., v., 456.

Again, there is nothing contained in the law of reason which a man who is normal in both intelligence and maturity may not find out by work and endeavor. We may sum this up by saying that the general principles of the law of reason are of such a character that it is not easy to find men who are ignorant of them. This rational law was formerly commonly called the law of nature, and by it is meant that law which human nature recognizes as that to which it is universally bound by reason. It is also for this reason properly called the law of reason. It includes all those matters which human beings quite obviously know or might know through the light of their natural understanding, to be becoming or unbecoming, virtuous or vicious, good or evil for them to do.

The proper observance of this law taught by reason cannot fail to be very beneficial to those who observe it. This is true because the whole world is so knit together that, so long as each part does the work which is unique and appropriate to it, that part conserves itself and other things as well. But on the other hand, if any important thing, such as the sun, the moon, or any of the heavenly bodies or elements, should ever cease to function, fail or swerve from its course, who would fail to realize that the result would be ruin both for the thing itself and whatever else depends upon it?

Is it then possible that man, who is not only the noblest creature in the world but also a true world in himself, could transgress the law of his nature without producing any kind of harm from doing so? No, it is not, for there is "tribulation and anguish, upon every soul of man that doeth evil."[6] Good is the result when all objects observe the type of action appropriate to their own nature, and evil is the result when they do not observe it. However, the good that results from the appropriate action of natural agents is not a reward, and the evil is not punishment. The reason for this is that, among the creatures of this world,

[6]Rom. 2. 9.

only man's observance of the law of his nature is righteousness, and only man's transgression is sin. This is because of the difference of the manner in which man observes or transgresses the law of his nature. His way of doing it is to observe voluntarily or to transgress voluntarily.

What we do against our will, or are forced to do, we are not appropriately said to do. That is because the motive that makes us do so does not lie in ourselves but outside of us, and carries us along as a wind does a feather in the air, while we do not even aid the force that drives us along. In cases of this kind, therefore, the evil which is done moves our compassion. The men who do evil under compulsion are pitied for it. They are wretchedly unhappy because of their acts, and do not merit blame for them. There are other cases where men do not act of their own free wills, although they are not constrained by external force. In these cases the acts are not done against men's wills, but without them. This is true where there is a loss of mind, where there is a lack of discretion and judgment. That is the reason that no one ever thinks that the injurious actions of the insane or half-wits ought to be punished.

Again, there are cases when we do things that are neither against our wills nor without our wills, and yet are not completely voluntary. In such cases we act voluntarily; and yet, although we might possibly do otherwise than we do, it would be very difficult to do otherwise than we do. When this is taken into consideration, one evil deed becomes more pardonable than another.

Finally, even though what we do is evil, it is the more pardonable as the emergency which incited it or the difficulty of doing otherwise is the greater,—except in those cases where we ourselves have created the necessity or the difficulty. It is no excuse, therefore, if a man commits incest when he is drunk, and then says that he was out of his mind; for he might have chosen whether he would have been out of his mind through drunkenness, or not.

Thus, rewards and punishments always presuppose something done voluntarily either well or ill. If there is no voluntary action, even though our acts result in good or evil to us, still the good is only a benefit and not a reward, and the harm is only an injury and not a punishment. The will is the source of all of man's action, and from the diverse intentions of the will arises, as a consequence, a variety of rewards and punishments. The rewards and punishments are meted out in accordance with the following rules, or others like unto them. If there is no will, then all acts are alike in merit. The thing which we did not do but would have done if we could have, is by common consent treated as if it had been done. By such rules men's actions are defined and judged as to whether they are worthy of reward or punishment.

Rewards and punishments are not meted out except at the hands of those who are above us and have the power to examine and judge our deeds. How it comes about that some men have the authority over other men's external actions we shall examine more carefully in the following pages. However, for the present moment we can all agree on one fact about our own inner conviction. When any man does good or evil, even when done in secret and known to no one but himself, his heart and conscience either approve or disapprove of him. Thus, the man either rejoices and his nature exults in a sure hope of reward, or else he grieves because of a sense of future punishment. And since the act was done in secret, the reward and the punishment can be expected from no other except from him who discerns and judges the very secrets of all hearts. Therefore, he is the only rewarder and revenger of all such actions, although not only of such actions, but all actions which break the law of nature, of which he is the author. That is the reason that the

Roman laws, called the Laws of the Twelve Tables, require an investigation of the inner inclinations which the eye of man cannot reach; and they threaten those who violate the Laws with nothing else except divine punishment.

CHAPTER VI

HUMAN LAWS AND THE BODY POLITIC

I hope that what we have previously said proves how irrational those are who think that religion and moral virtue are simply matters of opinion. They believe that it would really make no difference if we held the very opposite belief, and they think that we might do so without any injury to ourselves. But we have seen how nature itself teaches us laws and statutes by which to live. The laws, however, which we have mentioned thus far, constrain human beings as absolute obligations, even though they have no fixed fellowship or any solemn agreement among themselves as to what they should or should not do.

By himself, no man has the power to furnish himself with a sufficient supply of the things that are necessary for such a life as our nature desires, a life fit for the dignity of man. Therefore, in order to remedy the defects and imperfections of a life lived alone and by ourselves, we are naturally led to seek communion and fellowship with others. That is why in the very beginning men united themselves into civil societies, and as these societies could not exist without government, so government could not exist without a kind of law different from that which we have already mentioned.

Public societies rest on two foundations. The first of these is the natural inclination that drives all men to sociable life and fellowship. The second is a fixed arrangement, explicitly or secretly agreed upon, controlling men's manner of common life together. This fixed arrangement is called the law of the commonwealth. It is the very soul of the body politic, for the parts of the commonwealth are animated and held together by law, and the parts perform such actions as are required by the common good.

Those laws of the state which are decreed for the sake of external order and government are never correctly formulated unless they presuppose that the will of man is inwardly obstinate, rebellious, and disinclined to obey the sacred laws of his own nature. They are not correctly framed unless they assume that the depraved mind of man is little better than that of a wild beast. For this reason the laws provide that man's external actions be so ordered that even despite his waywardness they produce no hindrance to the common good for which societies are founded. Unless the laws do this they are not perfect.

Therefore, since human nature is of this sort, the law of nature requires some sort of government, but as there are many kinds of government nature does not bind us down to any one of them, but leaves us a free choice of them. At the beginning after a particular kind of government had been agreed upon by the group, it may have been that for the time being no further thought was given by those governed to the way in which they were governed, but those who ruled were allowed to use their wisdom and discretion as to how they governed. They continued until experience taught those who were ruled that this kind of government was not very convenient in every respect. Thus, the very thing which had been devised as a remedy for the chaos of individual life actually only increased the sore which it should have healed. People saw that life lived in accordance with one man's will became the cause of every man's misery. This forced them to devise laws so that everybody could see his duties before the time of action came, and could know the penalties for transgressing the laws before he acted.

Thus it was that the first laws that were promulgated contained that which is naturally good or evil, although the good or evil is more hidden than can be readily discerned by every man's present insight, unless he uses somewhat deeper reason and judgment. In this process of reasoning many persons would be ignorant of their duties, of which they are not now ignorant, if such things were not set down by law. That is because the discovery of the laws is difficult, and because it is easy to make many mistakes about them. If it were not for the laws, many would be ignorant of their duties who are not now, and many who know what they should do would nevertheless pretend that they did not, and would pretend that they were ignorant and stupid in order to excuse themselves. With the laws they cannot do that.

Most men prefer their own private good to anything else, and that is true even when their private good is sensual and stands opposed to the most divine good. Also, the duty that is prescribed to them by law cannot sufficiently gain the ascendency over them because the effort required to do good and the pleasure arising from evil make most humans disinterested in the good and more interested in the evil. Therefore, it always seems necessary to add rewards to the laws that are made for the good of man, so that, because of the reward, the good even with its difficulty of achievement will be more alluring than the evil is. And punishments are added which make the evil a thing more to be avoided, even though its attractiveness lures us to it. The general principle that *virtue is to be rewarded and vice is to be punished* is a rule of natural law, but the particular application of this law in terms of exact reward or exact punishment for a particular situation is a matter that has to be settled by those who make the law. It is a law of nature that theft should be punished, but the kind of punishment to be used is a matter of positive law, and the law ought to determine what shall be thought to be wise and suitable as a punishment of theft.

Natural law constrains us as a universal obligation; positive law does not do so. However, at this point we will not deal with all types of positive law, such as the kind of positive law which men impose upon themselves in the form of vows to God, contracts with men, and the like; but we will consider what is involved in the making of positive laws for the government of those who are united together in a civil society.

Laws not only teach us what is good, but they impose the good on us with authority, and therefore have in themselves a certain constraining force. However, to constrain men to do anything that is unsuitable seems unreasonable. Therefore, it is most necessary that only wise men be allowed to devise the laws which all men shall be forced to obey. Laws are matters of the highest consequence, and therefore men of merely ordinary capacity or merely commonplace judgment have not the ability to discern the things that are most appropriate for every kind and condition of government.

We cannot fail to realize how much our obedience to the laws depends upon the appropriateness of the positive law. If a man opposes the evil doers, even if he does so most justly, every one of them is offended at such opposition, storms at the reproof, and hates the man who would reform him. However, the same people who think it evil that people should tell them of their duties think it good and reasonable when they are told the same thing in terms of the law. The reason for this is that they assume that the law is completely impartial, and that it is not referring to them in particular. They think so because they believe that the law is like an oracle, based on wisdom and understanding.

Despite the fact that none but the wise should devise them, the laws do not take their constraining force from those who devise them, but from that power that gives them the strength of laws. What we said earlier about the power of government is also true of the power of making laws with which to govern. The power of the laws is that of God who has power over all. God has subjected all men to the natural law and by its means he has given to the whole of the group which makes up a given state the lawful power of making laws for that state. Thus, for any prince or potentate whatsoever—God excepted—to exercise this power merely of himself is no better than tyranny unless he has received an explicit commission directly from God or else has his authority derived originally from the consent of those persons upon whom he imposes the law.

Unless there is public sanction there is no law. There is approbation in cases where persons declare their assent by voice, sign, or act, but there is also sanction when representatives assent to it in the name of those whom they represent and do so by a right originally derived from those who are under it. That is the authority of parliaments, councils, and of governmental assemblies of that general type, for, although we are not personally present ourselves, still we give our assent to legislation through our representatives because they act as agents in our behalf. And even though the thing is done by others, that does not mean that their act is not our act, and that the act done does not obligate us as much as if we ourselves had done it in person.

Often when assent is given those who give it do not realize that they have done so, because it is not clear how they gave their consent. Let us take two instances where the consent is present but not obvious. First, suppose an absolute monarch commands his subjects to do that which seems good to him, his edict has the force of law whether his subjects approve of it or not. Then no consent seems involved, or in any way connected with the matter. Second, suppose there is a law which was accepted a long time ago and now is established by custom, and we keep it today and may not transgress it. In such a case, what consent was ever sought from us or required of us?

If we are to see how our assent is involved when an absolute monarch commands his subjects, or when ancient custom has the force of present law, we must note several things. First, it is not true that any men by nature have full and perfect power to rule over states. Therefore, if we, the governed, never give our assent, no man alive can rule over us. In fact, we do consent to be governed when that society of which we are a part has consented to be ruled over, and has never thereafter revoked that rule by universal agreement. The past legal acts of every man are valid as long as he lives. So likewise, the legal acts of a civil society done five hundred years ago are legally those of the members of that same society existing at the present. That is because corporations are immortal. Legally, we are alive in our predecessors, and they are still alive in us, their successors. Therefore, human laws of every kind are made valid by common consent.

CHAPTER VII

Supernatural Law and Human Felicity

WE have proved that everything except God has not only a possible perfection of nature but can receive some perfection from outside itself through the instrumentality of other things. From this it follows that there is nothing in the whole world, whether it be great or small, that may not add some sort of perfection to us, either by way of knowledge or by way of use. The perfection which may be achieved by our nature is appropriately called our good. It is called our sovereign good or blessedness when the highest degree of perfection is achieved. When this highest degree of perfection is achieved, nothing further can be desired. Therefore, when we have it our souls are fully contented and satisfied, and because they have it they rejoice and thirst no more.

Therefore, of the good things we desire, some of them we do not want for themselves but only because they can be used as instruments by which we can gain that which we do want. Riches are things that are desired in this way.

There is another kind of good, which is desired for itself but even so is not the ultimate goal at which we aim. Health, virtue, and knowledge are examples of this kind of good. Because with them alone we are not satisfied, they point beyond themselves to some further end as the goal of our desires. Even when we possess them our desires lead on to something beyond them. Thus we find goods linked together in the form of a chain. We labor to eat, and we eat to live, and we live to do good, and the good which we do is like seed sown for the sake of a future harvest, for "he that soweth to the Spirit shall of the Spirit reap life everlasting."[1]

[1] Gal. 6. 8.

Goods, however, are not linked together like a chain of infinite length. There is an ultimate goal of our desires. Suppose everything were desired for the sake of something else. Suppose there were no final good as the goal of our endeavors. Then there could be no assured purpose of our actions. That would mean that we would not know where we were going, and that our activity would be in vain. To put it more accurately, it would mean that we could not get anything done at all.

The assumption that there is no final goal of our endeavors is very much like the assumption that there is no first cause of our being. If we assume the first cause to be removed, then our persons would be entirely annihilated. And so if our purpose is removed our purposeful activity ceases.

Therefore, there must be something that is desired for itself alone and not for the sake of anything else. It is something desirable simply for itself and itself alone. It is absolute value because its very nature is repugnant to being desired as a means to something else or in relation to something else.

Absolute value is more than the highest we value as an end in itself; it has an excellency of its own. The ox and the ass desire their food. They do not ask what end the food serves. For them the food is an ultimate good, and is desired for itself. The reason for this is not the character of the good, but their imperfect nature which cannot desire food except as an end in itself. That is not because the food is really an absolute end, but because of the imperfection of the ox and the ass; for the absolute end which is desired simply for itself has an excellency which does not permit it to be referred in any manner beyond itself.

When we desire something which is relative to some goal beyond itself, we do not desire it absolutely, but rather as a means to the end which it serves. If we desire the good in itself, however, that desire knows no limits and is therefore infinite. Suppose, however, we desire a good as our highest good, and suppose that we desire it with an infinite desire. Suppose, however, that this good is not itself infinite. Then we do wrong in making it our goal or our purpose. That is what the people do who make wealth or honor or pleasure or any other thing gained in this world their highest goal or felicity. We miss our goal if we desire any thing as our final perfection when it is not.

Nothing may be infinitely desired but that good which is really infinite. That is because the better the thing is, the more desirable it is. Hence, the most desirable thing has an infinity of goodness; therefore, if anything that is desirable is infinite, that has to be the highest of all the things that we desire. But as no good is infinite but God, he is our felicity and our bliss.

More than this, desire tends to produce a union with that which is desired. Therefore, if we are blessed in him it is because we participate and join with him. Again, the mere possession of a good thing cannot make those who have it happy unless they enjoy the thing they have. Therefore, we are happy when we fully enjoy God as the object that satisfies the powers of our souls with everlasting delight. If we are so satisfied, then, even as men, through our union with God we live in some sense the life of God.

From this it follows that happiness is that state in which we attain, as far as it may be attained, the full possession of that which is desired for itself alone. Happiness is the condition which contains in itself preeminently the satisfaction of our desires and the highest degree of all our perfection. We cannot have this perfection in this life, for while we are in this world we are subject to many imperfections,—griefs of the body and defects of the mind. Even our very best acts are painful and the effort involved irksome. The pain and the irksomeness we have without intermission.

So the very actions especially suited to perfect us in this present life we cannot do continually. Because of our weariness, we are frequently forced to interrupt such actions from time to time. In the state of bliss, where our union with God will be complete, there will be no such weariness connected with our activities. When we are in entire union with him, every power and faculty of our minds capable of dealing with so glorious an object will express itself completely. The understanding and the will are the faculties suited to cooperate in union with God. Our understanding apprehends and cooperates with God as the sovereign truth which includes the rich treasures of all wisdom; our wills apprehend him as the sea of goodness, which when tasted causes us to thirst no more.

When we have not yet attained the object for which we wish, the will, driven by desire, moves toward the object; but when the will has once obtained the desired object, it functions, activated by love. It is as St. Augustine says, "The thirst of those who desire is changed into a sweet joy of those who taste and are satisfied."[2] In this present life we do love the things that are good, but their goodness is usually useful to us. But in the life to come we shall love that which is good in itself and good chiefly because of the beauty that it possesses. The soul is the kind of being whose actions are perfected by the love of the infinitely good. Hence, as it receives that which is absolutely good, it is also perfected by the supernatural emotions of joy, peace, and delight. All of these will be endless and everlasting.

The perfection we seek is of a three-fold kind. The first and most elemental is sensory. That consists of those things which simple biological life requires as necessary tools for the very existence of life itself or else as the beauty and cultivation of our animal existence. The second perfection is intellectual. It consists of those things which no being below the level of man is capable either of having or of being even acquainted with. The third perfection is spiritual and divine. It consists

[2] Aug., *de Trin.*, lib. ix.

of those things which supernatural means make us desire while on this earth, but we do not obtain them here.

Those who make sensory perfection the whole aim of their life are said by the Apostle to have no other God but their belly, and to "mind earthly things."[*] Those who desire to achieve intellectual perfection seek to excel especially in all those things which knowledge and virtue recommend to man. This includes the law of moral and political perfection.

The proof, however, that there is something higher than either sensory of intellectual virtue is the very character of human desire. By its very character it is unsatisfied if there is not some higher thing than sensory or intellectual objects to satisfy it. Human beings do not seem to be satisfied simply with either the preservation of physical life or the achievement of intellectual or civic honors. As a matter of fact, men desire and often quite industriously and earnestly pursue the very things which have no value for the mere preservation of life. The object of such a higher desire transcends both the senses and the power of reason. It is something divine and heavenly; and it is something for which we seek although we do not know directly what it is. However, it so incites our intense desire that all known delights and pleasures are laid aside, and they give place to the search for a desire which is only assumed to exist.

If the soul of man did nothing else but give him physical life, then the things that pertain to physical life would content him. We know that is true of other animals. They enjoy their physical life, and indicate their satisfaction with it by seeking nothing beyond it. Their very satisfaction is an acknowledgment that there is no higher good which is appropriate to them. With us, however, it is different. Suppose a man had all the perfections that belong to every man alive. Suppose he had all the beauty, riches, honors, knowledge, and virtues of all

[*]Phil. 3. 19.

men. Even if such a man possessed all of this he would still seek and would earnestly thirst for something beyond these human achievements and above them. Thus, human nature, even in this life upon earth, clearly claims and calls out for a more divine perfection than either the sensory or intellectual.

This highest kind of perfection is received by men in the form of a reward. Rewards always presuppose that such duties have been performed as deserved rewards. Our actions are, therefore, the appropriate natural means by which to attain blessedness. On the other hand, it is not possible for nature to find any other way that leads to salvation except that of duties performed in such a way as to be rewarded. However, if we examine our activities, and look back to all human actions from the very foundation of the world, can any one say, "My ways are pure"? Since all flesh is guilty of crimes which God has threatened with eternal punishment, how can any one be saved by doing that which merits salvation?

Therefore, either there can be no way of salvation, or there is a way that is supernatural. If there is a supernatural way, it could never have been conceived or imagined by man unless God himself had revealed it to man in an unusual manner. That is the reason we call it the mystery or secret way of salvation.

PART TWO

THE INCARNATION AND THE SACRAMENTS

CHAPTER VIII. The Scriptures and the Way of Salvation
CHAPTER IX. Prayer and Sacrament
CHAPTER X. The Personal Incarnation of the Son of God
CHAPTER XI. The Union of the Two Natures of Christ
CHAPTER XII. The Omnipresence of Christ
CHAPTER XIII. Participation in Christ
CHAPTER XIV. The Necessity of the Sacraments for Participation in Christ
CHAPTER XV. The Sacrament of Baptism
CHAPTER XVI. The Sacrament of the Body and Blood of Christ

CHAPTER VIII

THE SCRIPTURES AND THE WAY OF SALVATION

SINCE the life of all flesh is excluded from salvation through the natural way, the wisdom of God has revealed a mystical and supernatural way. This way directs us to eternal bliss by a course which is founded, not upon human merit, but upon the guiltiness of sin, and the condemnation and death that result from sin. Our way of salvation rests upon the tender compassion of God for us who are swallowed up in misery. It is a redemption from misery by the precious death and merit of a mighty Savior. It was he who said of himself, "I am the way."[1] Our Savior was the way which leads us from misery to bliss.

God himself prepared this supernatural way of salvation before all worlds. In the Gospel of St. John our Savior notes the way of supernatural duty which he has prescribed for us. He calls it *the work of God*,—"This is the work of God, that ye believe on him whom he hath sent."[2] That does not mean that God requires nothing more of us than mere belief if we are to obtain our highest happiness, for we cannot exclude a need for hope and love. It does mean, however, that without belief nothing else is of value, and it means that belief is the ground of hope and love.

The principal object of faith is the eternal truth which has discovered the treasuries of hidden wisdom in Christ. The highest object of hope is the eternal goodness which makes the dead alive through Christ. The final object of love is the incomprehensible beauty which shines in the face of Christ, the Son of the living God.

[1] Jn. 14. 6.
[2] Jn. 6. 29.

On earth the first beginning of these virtues is a faint apprehension of things not seen. In the world to come, the end of these virtues is the intuitive vision of God. On earth the second beginning of these virtues is the hesitant expectation of things that are far away and, up to this time, only heard of. In the world to come, this ends with a real and actual fruition of such glory as no tongue can express. On earth, the third beginning is a weak inclination of our heart directed upwards toward him whom we are not able to approach. In the world to come, the end of that inclination is an endless union with God. The mystery of this union is higher than the highest reaches of human thought.

Faith, hope, and love do not spring from the natural but from the supernatural. Without them there can be no salvation, and yet they are never mentioned except in that law which God himself has revealed from heaven. In this world there is no certain truth about any one of the three. The only certainty we have about them has been supernaturally received from the mouth of the eternal God.

The laws about faith, hope, and love are supernatural. The way in which they are delivered to man is supernatural, because that way is divine; the laws themselves are supernatural, because they are not laws of nature but the voluntary appointments of God to supplement the laws of nature. Their purpose is to correct the defects of nature. However, although these supernatural duties are our obligations, they do not cancel natural duties and make them superfluous. Both are, therefore, necessary for our eternal salvation, although the natural way needs supplementation by the supernatural way, and the supernatural way presupposes the natural way.

We see that there must be some way of knowing the things just mentioned as necessary for salvation. Many of them, however, cannot be discovered by the light of nature, and so, if there is no supernatural knowledge, everyone is excluded from salvation. To assume that would be very cruel; and we believe that there is such supernatural knowledge, and that God has revealed to us a way of life which is our salvation.

"God, who at sundry times and in divers manners spake in time past"[a] to the sons of men, gave them a knowledge of salvation. He has not only taught the Church by speech, but he has done so by writing. He used writing to make his revelations to this world more permanent and certain than they otherwise would have been. Anything recorded by pen on paper is of more permanence and assurance than the merely oral memorials which use no pen but a tongue, and no book but the ear of man.

Each book of Scripture was written on a particular occasion and for a particular purpose. The content of every book of Scripture is relevant to the special purpose for which it was written. For that reason each book of Holy Scripture uses every type of truth necessary to present the purpose the book reveals. And that is the case, whether the truth is natural, historical, foreign, or supernatural.

We have given sufficient reason to conclude that everything necessary for salvation must be made known to us, and that God has for that reason revealed his will. Otherwise, men could not have known what was necessary for their salvation. The fact that God has ceased to speak to the world since the publication of the Gospel of Jesus Christ and its delivery to us in writing is an obvious indication that the way of salvation is now sufficiently revealed to us, and that we do not need any further instruction besides that which God has already given us.

The essential meaning of the whole New Testament is summed up in St. John's words about the purpose of his own Gospel, "These are written, that ye might believe that Jesus is the Christ, the Son of God; and that believing ye might have

[a] Heb. I. I.

life through his name."⁴ The essential meaning of the Old Testament is given to us by St. Paul in his letter to Timothy, "The Holy Scriptures . . . are able to make thee wise unto salvation."⁵ The general purpose of both the Old and the New Testament is the same. The difference between them is to be found in the fact that the Old Testament made us wise by instructing us about the salvation that was to come through Christ the Savior, while the New Testament makes us wise by instructing us that Christ the Savior has come, and that Jesus, who was crucified by the Jews, and who was raised up from the dead by God, is that Christ.

Therefore, when St. Paul told Timothy that the Old Testament could "make him wise unto salvation", he did not mean that the Old Testament by itself was sufficient for those who have lived since the publication of the New Testament. He writes to Timothy with the presupposition that Timothy already knows the doctrine of Christ, for, just before the words we have quoted, he says, "Continue thou in the things which thou hast learned and hast been assured of, knowing of whom thou hast learned them."⁶ Although St. Paul granted that the Old Testament could make Timothy "wise to salvation", he adds the qualification "through faith which is in Christ Jesus."⁷

Therefore, unless it is completed by the New Testament, the Old Testament cannot by itself do as much for us as the Apostle says it will. The praise of the Old Testament in such high terms presupposes its completion in the New. The reason for this is that the Old Testament only foreshadows the New Testament teaching of redemption through Christ; but it is the New Testament that reveals that redemption. St. Paul's praise of the Old Testament presupposes an acceptance of the Gospel

⁴Jn. 20. 31.
⁵2 Tim. 3. 15.
⁶2 Tim. 3. 14.
⁷2 Tim. 3. 15.

of Christ as giving the meaning of that which is foreshadowed in the Old Testament.

In a similar way, when we praise the complete sufficiency of the whole body of Scripture, we too have a presupposition. We presuppose that the light of nature is a necessary background for the understanding of Holy Scriptures; and although we grant that there is a necessity of a diviner light than that of the light of nature, we do not mean that the light of nature is unnecessary.

There is, therefore, no defect in the Scripture; and its perfection is such that it both perfects and completes the natural understanding. There is no duty necessary for life in the Church of God that is not revealed by the light of the natural understanding completed by the revelation of Holy Scripture. The Holy Scriptures supplement our natural knowledge; and there is no good work required by God which is not taught to us, either by our natural understanding or by the Scriptures. Thus, these two together give us all needful instruction for all our obligations whether they be natural or supernatural, and whether they be duties to men simply as men, or men united together in some sort of a society. The light of nature is not sufficient for our everlasting felicity, nor is Scripture alone sufficient for it. The two of them together, however, give us complete knowledge of all that is necessary for it, and we do not need any other knowledge than that supplied by them working in conjunction.

God has given us our senses so that we can see with them the things that we need in this present life. He has given us reason because our senses cannot give us information about many things that we should know about this present life and about the life to come. Last of all, he has given us heavenly aid through prophetic revelation, and it has opened up those hidden mysteries that reason has never been able to discover, or even to have known as necessary for our everlasting good. It is our duty to use all of these precious gifts to the honor and glory of the One who gave them all to us. We ought also to seek by every means in our power to know what the will of God is, what is righteous in his sight, what he considers as holy, perfect and good; and then we ought to do all of this.

CHAPTER IX

Prayer and Sacrament

THAT the angels continually carry messages between the throne of God in heaven and the Church militant on earth, is most clearly proved by the two spiritual exercises of instruction and prayer. The gathering of the Church together to learn is the reception of angels that have descended from God; and prayer is the dispatching of angels that ascend to God. Both God's holy influence upon us and our holy desires rising to him are like so many angels carrying messages between him and us. As instruction makes us realize that God is our supreme truth, so prayer confirms our realization that he is our sovereign good.

There is, however, another aspect of prayer. All lower causes in the world are dependent on God as the highest cause. The higher in rank any cause is, the more it desires to impart virtue to the things beneath it. Therefore, there is no other kind of service we do or find to do which is more acceptable to God than prayer. It is prayer that reveals our agreement with God, for when we pray we desire the very thing that delights him most.

It is usual to call the services we render to God by the name of prayer. We have no other reason for doing that, I suppose, except the desire to prove that religion knows no duty acceptable to God which is not assumed when we make a devout supplication in his name. Prayers are the "calves of our lips",[1] the sacrificial offerings; they are the very gracious and sweet odors of burnt offerings. They are rich presents and gifts which "come up for a memorial before God."[2] They are the best

[1] Hos. 14. 2.
[2] Acts 10. 4.

possible proof of our dutiful affection; and they are the most authentic means for purchasing all favors at the hands of God.

What can we give to others more easily and yet more fruitfully than our prayers? If we give of our counsel, it is only the uninstructed who need it. If we give alms, it is only the poor who are aided. However, if we use prayer, every kind of man is aided. Also, any other duty can be performed only as time and opportunity make necessary; but prayer is suitable at any time. Suppose we can do nothing else for a man except pray for him. Suppose his malice or unkindness prevents him from accepting any other good at our hands. Even so, we can always pray for him, and he can never refuse us that right. That is the reason that Samuel, when he spoke to a very ungrateful people, a people weary of the benefits of his just government over them, said, "God forbid that I should sin against the Lord in ceasing to pray for you."[8] Prayer is the very beginning of a righteous life; and its very end as well.

Here on earth we have very little knowledge about the things that are done in heaven. However, we do know this much about the saints above: we know that they pray. Prayer is something done both by the Church militant and by the Church triumphant; it is something done by both men and angels. Therefore, we should realize that the time spent in the exercise of prayer is celestial and divine. That is the reason that those most helpful visits made by angels sent by God above to men below have taken place when men were praying; and that was the most natural time for them to take place.

The prayers of the just are always acceptable to God; but the just do not always receive the things for which they pray. Suppose we identify faith with the valid certainty that we shall receive what we request in our prayers. Then if we do not get what we ask for, that would be a clear indication that we were not correct in our confidence about the answer to our prayer.

[8] 1 Sam. 12. 23.

As a consequence, since the prayer involved a false certainty about future events, it was a prayer made to God without faith, for we identified faith with valid certainty. For that reason God would abhor a prayer without valid confidence. If we remember how many prayers of the saints failed to obtain the particular thing for which they asked, we see how absurd such an assumption is.

God's faithful people have the comfort of knowing that without doubt they receive those requests that accord with his will. The things that accord with his will are those that produce the glory of God and the everlasting good of the one who prays. It is not the purpose of any virtuous man either to seek or to desire to obtain anything that would be injurious either to the glory of God or to the everlasting good of the virtuous man himself. That is the reason that our Lord and Savior prayed in his agony, "O my Father, if it be possible."[4] When we pray on similar occasions we do not always use our Lord's words, but we imply them, "Nevertheless not as I will, but as thou wilt."[5]

Even if our petition is not in accord with God's will, and there are hidden obstacles and reasons that prevent the thing for which we pray being granted to us,[6] still the prayer itself is a pleasing sacrifice to God. Our prayers are both acceptable to God and receive some reward from him. Sinners are really refused when they seem to get what they ask for in their prayers. Those who are faithful, on the other hand, succeed best when they seem to be denied their request. That is because it is often for their good that their requests are not granted. St. Augustine says, "In his anger, our Lord God has granted the requests of some impatient men. On the other hand, in his favor and mercy he did not grant the Apostle Paul's request."[7]

There is no doubt that in everything we should conform our

[4] Mat. 26. 39.
[5] Ibid.
[6] 2 Cor. 12. 7-9.
[7] Migne, S. L. xxxiii, 504.

wills to that of God. Otherwise, everything we do is sinful. Of ourselves we are prone to sin, and the only way we have of straightening our paths is that of following the rule of his will whose path naturally is right. If the eye, the hand, and the foot do what is commanded by the will, they may be the instruments of sin; yet the sin committed is that of the will that commands them, and not the sin of the members. It is not their sin because nature has made eye, hand and foot the absolute subjects of the will of the man whose organs they are; and the man is the lord of his own body.

Just as the body is subject to the will of the man whose body it is, so man's will is subject to the will of God. That is because it is right and proper that the higher should guide and command the lower. There is, however, a difference in the subjection of the body to the will of the man whose body it is, and the subjection of the human will to God. The subjection of the body to the will of the man is the result of natural necessity; the subjection of the will of a man to the will of God is voluntary.

Therefore, we need some sort of direction as a guide for our wills and our desires, so that they may be correctly conformed to God's will. That does not mean that we should always will to do the same thing that God intends to do; it does mean that our wills should be conformed to his purpose for man. For example, it may be that he wishes the death of certain persons, yet if we did not wish their long continuance of life, it would be an unnatural thing for us.

Suppose the object of our prayers is a thing that is both good in itself and not forbidden of God. Suppose the end which we desire is virtuous, and seems to be most holy. Suppose the source of our affection for the thing we desire is love, and suppose our acts declare a pious desire and prayer. Suppose we are praying that all men may find mercy, and we do this because we know that when we pray for all men alive we are exhibiting towards them the same love which our Lord Jesus Christ had for them all. He knew as God who were his own; yet as a man he tasted death for the good of all men. When we pray, therefore, for God's mercy for all men, we are not opposing the will of God as the recognized rule of all our actions; and that is true, even if his unknown decrees are opposed to our petitions. Even though we did understand his purpose, which we certainly do not, yet all that is required of us is that we are content to agree with God's will. And as for ourselves, our earnest desire should be that we are willing to submit our wills to his will.

We have spoken of instruction and we have spoken of prayer. As teaching makes us realize that God is supreme truth, and prayer confirms our recognition that he is our sovereign Good, both instruction and prayer are our duties and obligations. They serve as the elements or principles of all else including the sacraments themselves.

The Church is the very mother of our new birth. We are born of her, and from her we receive nourishment. Therefore, everyone that we think is born of God is regenerated by the ministry of the Church and in this process the seed of regeneration is not only the word but the sacraments, for both have generative power and influence.

In their writing, the early Fathers usually use the term sacrament to denote all the articles peculiar to the Christian faith. They use it to denote all those duties of religion that contain something that sense or natural reason cannot understand. However, we will restrict the use of the word to two important divine ceremonies.

A sacrament is a ceremony which has two aspects, the matter of the ceremony, which is visible, and something else of a hidden nature which really makes the ceremony into a sacrament. We all admire and honor the holy sacraments, not because of the service that we render to God in receiving them, but because of the value of that sacred and hidden gift which God gives to us through them. A sacrament has the character of a sacrament because of the supernatural gift bestowed through it, for it is such a gift as only God can bestow. Therefore, it is only the Church that can administer those ceremonies as sacraments which the Church alone considers the sacraments.

When we deal with the sacraments we cannot understand them unless we observe in them two aspects, (1) their vital action, and (2) the form of administration as the means of producing that action. The vital action is what makes the sacraments necessary, and so we cannot understand the source of their necessity unless we know how the intended result is produced by them. When we say that the sacraments are visible signs of an invisible grace, we are really saying that grace is actually the very purpose for which these heavenly mysteries were instituted, and that, despite many other features in them, their matter is of such a character as to portray their purpose. But even though this much is clear, we do not escape a certain obscurity about how the result is obtained unless we understand quite clearly what is the particular grace that is the end which the given sacrament achieves, and the manner of operation necessary to obtain that result.

It is true that the sacraments are ceremonies that are used only in this world and not in heaven; but they do refer to a far better life than this, and are therefore accompanied with "the grace of God that bringeth salvation."* The sacraments are powerful instruments, and by means of them God imparts to us the grace that leads to eternal life. Our natural life consists in the union of body with soul; our supernatural life consists in the union of our soul with God. There is no union of God and man without a connection which is both God and man, and acts as a link between the two of them. That link is Christ, and, therefore, it is necessary that we consider first how God is in Christ, and second, how Christ is in us; and third, how the sacraments act as instruments that make us partakers of Christ.

*Tit. 2. 11.

CHAPTER X

THE PERSONAL INCARNATION OF THE SON OF GOD

"THE Lord our God is one Lord."[1] He is an indivisible unity; but even so, he is a Trinity, and in him we adore the Father as unbegotten, we glorify the consubstantial Word who is his only begotten Son, and we bless and exalt the co-essential Spirit who proceeds from both the Father and the Son. The Father is underived; the Son is begotten of the Father, and the Spirit proceeds from them both. Each of them can be distinguished from the other two by his own distinct property. The substance of God, together with the property of unbegottenness, makes up the Person of the Father. The same substance, together with the property of begottenness of the Father, makes up the Person of the Son. The same substance, added to the property of procession from the other two Persons, makes up the Person of the Holy Ghost. Each one of the Persons involves the substance of God, which is one and the same for all three. However, each Person has a property of his own, which makes him really different from the other two.

God became man, but it was not the Person of the Father or the Person of the Spirit that was "made flesh," but the Person of the Son. We should not think that either the Father or the Spirit became man; St. Peter confessed to Christ, "Thou art the Christ, the Son of the living God."[2] St. John's exposition is also plain, "And the Word was made flesh."[3] As St. John Damascus said, "The Father and the Holy Ghost had nothing to do with the incarnation of the Word, except as they gave their approbation and assent."[4]

[1] Deut. 6. 4.
[2] Mat. 16. 16.
[3] Jn. 1. 14.
[4] Damasc. Migne, S. G. xciv. 1028.

However, the Word is very God, and so we must be very careful lest we exclude the substance of God from the incarnation. If we did so, we would deny that the Incarnate Son of God was very God; for without doubt the very Nature of God himself is incarnate in the Person of the Son, and so the divine Nature has assumed flesh. That is the reason that the incarnation must be attributed to only one Person of the Trinity; but on the other hand, it cannot be denied that the Naure which is common to the three Persons of the Trinity was incarnate.

There is a reason for such an incomprehensible mystery. It seems appropriate that we should honor the Creator of the world as its Savior. On the other hand, in his wisdom, God has thought it befitting that man should save himself. Suppose we say nothing of the love and mercy of God for men, which in the incarnation are so marvelous that neither men nor angels can look upon them without a certain kind of heavenly amazement. Even so, because the Creator of the world must be its Savior, and yet man must save himself, we have a sufficient reason why divine Nature should assume human nature, so that God might be "in Christ, reconciling the world unto himself."[5]

There is also a reason why the Son, rather than either the Father or the Holy Ghost, should be made man. It would not have been possible for us who are by nature the children of wrath to become the adopted sons of God unless his natural Son had become a Mediator between him and us. "It became him, for whom are all things, and by whom are all things,"[6] to be the way of salvation for us all. In this way the creation and the restoration of the world were carried out by the same Person. It was impossible to save the world without the incarnation of the Son of God. When we say it was impossible we do not mean a simple impossibility, but an impossibility which had its foundation in the fact that God did not wish the world to be saved except through the death of his own Son. Therefore,

[5] 2 Cor. 5. 19.
[6] Heb. 2. 10.

the Son assumed our flesh, and by his incarnation made our flesh into his own flesh. Thus, he took something that was ours and made it his, and this flesh that was now his own was something he could offer to God in our behalf.

Christ assumed our manhood, and because he was man he could die the death to which he humbled himself. It is his manhood that makes possible his compassion and his pity, and thus it is that his rule, even in the kingdom of heaven, is a thing that is so lovable. Without our nature, he could not have suffered on earth for the sins of the world; but with it he makes intercession to God for sinners, and rules over all men with a true, a natural, and a tender mercy.

"The Word was made flesh and dwelt among us."[7] The Word, or the wisdom of God, did not wish to be incarnate in one human person. If that had happened, that one person would have been exalted, and no other persons would have been. The Word, or wisdom, did not do that; but he made his habitation "among us," that is, in manhood in general. That is so that he might save many men. Therefore, he built his dwelling place in that nature which is common to us all.

The seeds of herbs and plants are not yet what they will be when they have grown into matured herbs and plants. While they are still seeds they are potentially herbs and plants, and not yet actually such. Suppose the Son of God had become incarnate in a man already matured and perfected. In that case, there would necessarily be two persons in Christ,—the Person who assumed the other person, and the person who was assumed. Actually, the Son of God did not assume a man's person to be united with his own, but he did assume man's nature to be united with his own Person.

Therefore, he took, for the incarnation, the seed of Abraham, the very original element of our nature, before it had any personal human existence. The flesh of Jesus Christ and the union

[7] Jn. 1. 14.

of flesh with God began to exist at the same instant. The creation of the flesh and the assumption of the flesh were one act. Christ has only one personal existence, and that has been from all eternity. Because he assumed only the nature of man for his incarnation, and not a human person, Christ was one and only one Person. His Person only changed the form of its existence; his Person had existed previously only in the glory of the Son of God, and now it exists in the garments of our flesh.

Christ has no personal existence except that of the eternal Son of God. Therefore, even those things that belong to the human nature of Christ must be predicated of the Person of the Son of God. For example, from the standpoint of the flesh, he was born of the Virgin Mary, baptised of John in the River Jordan, was judged by Pontius Pilate, and was executed by the Jews. We cannot really say that the Virgin bore the nature of man, or that John baptised the nature of man, or that the Jews crucified the nature of man. All of these facts,—his baptism, his judgment, his death,—are personal attributes; and therefore his Person is the subject of all of them. However, his human nature is that which makes it possible for his Person to have such attributes.

Christ is a Person who is both God and man; but he is not the fusion of two persons into one. He is not God and man in the same sense; but he is God because he is personally the Son of God, and he is man because he actually has a nature which is that of the children of men. Therefore, as Paschasius says, Christ, as God in man, "is a two-fold substance, not a two-fold Person. That is because one Person, the divine Person, extinguishes the human person; but the human nature does not become extinct when united with the divine Nature."[9] His own divine Person as Son of God would not allow him to acquire a human person. However, when he assumed human nature, the

[9] Migne, S. L. lxii. 29.

Nature he had before the incarnation and the human nature which he assumed both continued. Therefore, no person was born of the Virgin Mary except the Son of God; no person was condemned but the Son of God; and no person was crucified but him. The infinite worth of the Son of God is the only true basis for all that we believe about life and salvation gained for us through the acts and the sufferings of Jesus Christ as man.

From the moment of their first union, these two natures of Christ have been, and always will be, inseparable. Even when our Lord's soul left the tabernacle of his body, his Deity did not leave either his body or his soul. If his Deity had forsaken either his body or his soul, we could not validly hold that either the Person of Christ was buried, or the Person of Christ rose from the dead. If the body had been separated from the Word, the Word could not rightly be termed the Person of Christ. Also, we cannot say that the Son of God arose if the body, even while in the tomb, was not his body. The soul must have also been his soul, and must have arisen with him from the tomb. The true Person of Christ is therefore one and the same. His body only was placed in the grave, because his soul was separated from his body at his death. However, despite the separation of body and soul in death, his Deity was inseparably united to both body and soul by a personal union.

CHAPTER XI

The Union of the Two Natures of Christ

THE two natures of Christ are the sources of everything that he has done. He did some things, therefore, as God, because his Deity is the only source from which they flow; he did some things as man, because they flow from his human nature alone. Still other things he did as both God and man, because both natures are sources of these acts.

It is true that the properties of each of his natures belong only to that nature whose properties they are. Therefore, Christ as God cannot be the same thing as Christ as man. Even so, both natures may very well work together to produce a single effect. In such a case, Christ may be said to do a single thing both as God and man. Therefore, let us lay down a necessary rule for the simplest solution of all doubts and questions about the union of the natures of Christ: the two natures often function in cooperation; they always function in association; but they never participate in each other's nature in such a way that the properties of one nature fuse with those of the other.

This rule helps us to understand what St. John Damascus[1] says about the *communicatio idiomatum*, or the substitution of properties in our descriptions of Christ. Thus, we attribute properties to him as God which belong to him as man, and we attribute properties to him as man which belong to him as God. The reason for this is the association of the two natures in one Person. There is a sense in which the two natures of Christ are said to impart their properties to each other; but even so, not in the abstract but in the concrete, so that the qualities of God-

[1] Migne, S. G. xciv. 1000.

head are attributed not to humanity but to man, and the qualies of manhood not to Deity but to God.

We can say that the Son of God created the world, and the Son of Man saved it by his death; or we can say that the Son of Man created the world, and the Son of God died to save it. However, if we do attribute to God something that belongs to the manhood of Christ, or if we attribute to man something that belongs to his Deity, we understand by the name man and the name God neither one nature nor the other, but the whole Person of Christ, in whom both natures exist together.

Let us take two examples of "the substitution of properties." The Apostle Paul said that the Jews crucified the Lord of Glory; and Christ as man spoke of the Son of Man as in heaven at that very same moment he as Son of Man was saying that on earth. In both of these cases there is in our use of words a *communicatio idiomatum*. In the case of the words of St. Paul, he attributes death to the Lord of Glory, and we know that the divine Nature cannot die. In the case of Christ's own words, he asserts omnipresence as characteristic of man; and yet human nature is not capable of omnipresence. Therefore, when St. Paul says "the Lord of Glory",[2] he means the whole Person of Christ. for the whole Person of Christ was Lord of Glory, and was crucified. However, he did not suffer death as Lord of Glory, but as man. When Christ speaks of the Son of Man being in heaven, it is the whole Person of Christ of whom he speaks. The Person of Christ was man on earth, and also as Lord of Glory he filled all heaven with his glorious presence. However, he did not fill the heaven by virtue of being the Son of Man but by virtue of being the Lord of Glory.

We have shown that both of the natures of Christ keep their own distinct properties. If we are to understand what each nature receives from the other, we must recognize that Christ is a recipient in three ways. First of all, Christ has received

[2] 1 Cor. 2. 8.

his eternal Sonship. Second, his human nature has received the honor of union with Deity. Third, his human nature has received many preeminent graces from the Deity coupled with it. Thus, Christ has had three gifts bestowed upon him: the gift of eternal generation, the gift of union with God, and the gift of unction.

Let us begin by considering the first gift, the gift of eternal generation. In this gift Christ received from the Father that nature which came from the Father, and is the Father's own substance, underived from anything else. Whatever gives being to something else is the father of that which is born of it, and everything that proceeds from an origin is the son of that out of which it springs. The Father is the origin of that Deity which Christ has, and in that sense, Christ is not the origin but an offspring. Christ is God because he is "of God,"[3] and Christ is Light because he is "of Light."[4] Consequently, whatever Christ has in common with his heavenly Father is a heavenly gift. This gift is a natural and eternal gift, and not a gift of benevolence and favor as the gifts of union and unction are.

Let us consider the second gift, which is the union of Deity with manhood. This is an act of God's kindness and favor, because God showed the greatest kindness to man when he permitted the union of the Person of his only begotten Son with man's nature. "The Father loveth the Son,"[5] and loves him not only as Deity but as man. He loves the Son as Son of Man, and by the gift of Deity to manhood he has given to man power over all things.[6]

Therefore, "God also hath highly exalted him, and given him a name which is above every name."[7] "As the Father hath life in himself; so hath he given to the Son to have life in

---

[3] Nicene Creed.
[4] Ibid.
[5] Jn. 3. 35.
[6] Ibid.
[7] Phil. 2. 9.

himself,"[a] and that as a gift of his Father. The gift that makes Christ a fountain of life is the conjunction of the Nature of God with the nature of man in the Person of Christ. As Christ said to the woman of Samaria, "If thou knewest the gift of God, and who it is that saith to thee, Give me to drink; thou wouldst have asked of him, and he would have given thee living water."[9] Therefore, when God united flesh with Deity he gave man a gift of the highest kindness and favor. The power of this kindness makes Christ, as man, actually God; and thus a creature is raised above the dignity of all creatures, and has all other creatures beneath him.

This remarkable union of God with man cannot possibly change the Nature of God because God cannot change. However, despite the fact that the Word as God cannot change his nature, it is possible that he should change his manner of existence when he was made flesh, even though he had not had that type of existence before. However, the properties of the Word were the same as they always had been. The incarnation of the Son of God was merely a union and not a fusion, and in this union perfection was added to manhood as the weaker nature, but nothing was added to God as the nobler Nature.

Why, then, did the Son of God assume manhood? What did he gain by doing it? The answer is that by becoming man he was able to undertake lower tasks than he could have as Son of God. The only advantage that he gained for himself was the power of suffering loss and detriment for the good of others.

Let us now consider the third gift, the grace of unction. The soul and body of Christ united with human nature in general rather than a particular man. In this union of God with man, Deity so influenced generic human nature that its powers, virtues, and qualities were heightened beyond their natural capacities. A sword which has been heated until it is red hot not

[a] Jn. 5. 26.
[9] Jn. 4. 10.

only cuts because of the sharpness which it has as a sword, but it also burns because of the heat it has from the fire. In like manner, the Deity of Christ makes that nature of man, which he assumed, to do more than we can ever understand.

God gave to the manhood of Christ every power except those of God's own essential properties. God gave manhood in Christ every perfection which human nature can receive. Of course, there were limits to this gift, and they were controlled by necessities of that order which in his love and mercy he has made for man. The light of God either contracted or expanded in conformity with the requirements of God's mystical administration. The light of Deity was contracted when our Lord was tempted, when he was crucified, and when he was dying; but its illumination was expanded when he rose from the dead, when he ascended into the heavens.

This helps us to understand the light that illuminated the faculties of the soul of Christ. His human nature was so close to his divine Nature that he could not choose but know all the things which God did. Therefore, by very necessity he was endowed with all the treasures of wisdom and knowledge; but he did not have that infinite knowledge peculiar to Deity. Even in this life on earth, the soul of Christ saw the face of God. The visible presence of Deity filled him with all sorts of favors and virtues, and such unparalleled perfection as that spoken of by the Apostle, "Wherefore God, even thy God, hath anointed thee with the oil of gladness above thy fellows."[10]

God in Christ has not only glorified the nobler part of human nature, but also the lower part of our nature, the very bodily substance of man. We must remember once more what we said above, that the degrees of influence of the Deity on human nature are in relation to God's purposes and plans. That is the reason that the body of Christ was by nature corruptible and did not have the gift of everlasting immunity from death, suf-

[10] Ps. 45. 7. (Prayer Bk. Vers.); Heb. 1. 9.

fering, and decay. So it remained until it was used for an offering and was slain for sin. Then, and then only, for righteousness' sake, it was restored to life with the certainty that it would continue forever. That is the reason that the very glorified body of Christ retained the scars and the marks of its former mortality.

CHAPTER XII

The Omnipresence of Christ

WE have spoken of the Person of Jesus Christ, his two natures, and the union of the two in one Person. We have asserted what each one of the natures is and what it does, and what each receives from the other. We have made clear that God in Christ is that general medicine that cures the world, and that Christ in us is our reception of this medicine. By this medicine, each one of us is individually cured because Christ's incarnation and passion are of no value to any man if he is not a partaker of Christ. It is also true that we cannot participate in Christ without Christ's presence. For that reason we will briefly consider the character of Christ's presence in our lives, and thus we can better understand how we are made partakers of Christ, both in other ways and in the sacraments themselves.

Everything that exists is either finite or infinite; and these alternatives are so mutually exclusive that nothing that is infinite can be finite, and nothing that is finite can be infinite. This mutual exclusion is true of substances, natures, and qualities; and so both the world and everything in the world are bounded. Every result that is produced from the world or the things in it is also limited, and all the powers and capacities by which the result is produced are likewise limited. That means that whatever they do, whatever they can do, and whatever they are, are all limited. The limitation of each created thing is both the perfection and the preservation of that thing. Measure perfects everything because everything exists for some purpose, and a given thing cannot achieve a purpose which is not proportionate to that thing; and excess and defect are a matter of proportion.

The presence of a thing is the result of the kind of substance it is; and, because God's very substance is infinite, it is impossible for God to withdraw his presence from anything. Since omnipresence is a property of an infinite and incomprehensible substance, the question of Christ's omnipresence is a matter of a natural property that belongs to the Deity of Christ. The Deity of Christ is shared by him as a common property with the Father and the Holy Ghost; and so omnipresence is a matter of the Deity, not the humanity, of Christ. Hence, no part of Christ that is limited or created can possibly be omnipresent, and that means that Christ as soul and body, Christ as man, cannot be omnipresent, for his limitations and restraints indicate the nature of which they are attributes.

As man, Christ has a limited nature and is spatially located; for, if Christ as man were omnipresent, such omnipresence would not result from his manhood, but from either the grace of his union with the Deity, or the grace of unction received from Deity. However, we have already proved conclusively that in the union of the two natures in Christ, the properties of each nature are imparted to the one Person of Christ, and yet are not transferred to each other. We also proved that each of the natures united with the other in the Person of Christ continues to be the very same nature which it was before it was thus united in him. Even the grace of unction does not take away from Christ the nature and substance of man; and unction does not cause his soul and body to be of a different sort from ours. This is true even though it is the grace of unction which furnishes the gifts and virtues which exalt Christ above other men and make him actually a man more excellent than we are. Supernatural gifts exalt human nature, but do not extinguish the nature to which they are given.

The only presence that the substance of the body of Christ has or can have is local. Christ's body was not visible everywhere when he was on earth; it did not suffer death everywhere; it was not buried everywhere; and at the present moment, as an exalted body in heaven, it is not present everywhere.

The only convincing proof that Christ had an actual body is the evidence furnished by the natural properties of a body, and among the properties of a natural body, definite and local presence are the chief. "Have no doubt or question," says St. Augustine, "but that the man Christ Jesus is now in that very place from which he shall come again in the same form and substance of flesh which he took up to heaven. He did not take away the nature of that body, but only gave it immortality, and if it has the true form as a body, it cannot be spread out everywhere. When we maintain the Deity of the one who is man, we must be careful to leave him the true bodily substance of man."[1] St. Augustine thinks that if we make that majestical body of Christ omnipresent, we cause it to lose the substance of a real body.

Christ's human substance itself is naturally absent from earth; his soul and body are not on earth but in heaven. Yet, in three manners, his manhood is everywhere present. First, Christ's manhood has universal presence by means of conjunction. Because his manhood is joined inseparably with that personal Word which by his very divine essence is omnipresent, the human nature which cannot in itself have universal presence has it too. However, the manhood of Christ is not omnipresent, for only the connection of manhood with Deity is omnipresent; and thus the humanity is tied down to a certain place, and only the conjunction is omnipresent.

Second, the universality of the presence of Christ's manhood may also be seen in the cooperation of his manhood with his Deity, and this cooperation is complete. And that Deity of Christ, which before our Lord's incarnation did everything without man, does nothing now without the presence or activity of the human nature which the Deity has assumed. Christ, as man, has all power given him both in heaven and on earth. It is as man, as well as God, that he has supreme rule over

[1] Migne, S. L. xxxiii. 835.

both the living and the dead; and that is the meaning of his ascension to heaven and his session at the right hand of God.

The session at the right hand of God is the actual exercise of that rule in which the manhood of Christ is joined with, and works with, the Deity of the Son of God. That does not mean that before his ascension his manhood did not have the same power that it had after the ascension, but it does mean that the complete use of that power was suspended while he was on earth. It simply means that he began to govern only after he had laid aside the humility which hid his majesty like a veil.

It was only after he arose from the dead that God "set him at his own right hand in the heavenly places, far above all principality, and power, and might, and dominion, and every name that is named, not only in this world, but also in that which is to come," and "put all things under his feet."[2] God has appointed him as head of the Church, which is Christ's body, "the fullness of him that filleth all in all."[3] There will come a time when Christ will surrender this spiritual rule over us in this present world, and will give the world back to his Father who gave it to him. That means that he will then cease to govern because there will no longer be a Church militant on earth which he can govern.

Christ rules both as God and as man. He rules as God because he is present everywhere with everything that exists; he rules as man because he cooperates with that Deity which by its very nature is present everywhere. The principal powers of the soul of man are his will and his understanding. As man, Christ has both these powers; and it is by virtue of these two powers that the humanity of Christ works in all things. It happens in this fashion: the will of Christ's humanity assents to all that his Deity does, and the intellect of his humanity knows what his Deity does. Thus, because as a man he knows

[2] Eph. 1. 20-22.
[3] Eph. 1. 23.

and assents to everything which the Deity as the other Nature does, his humanity in a sense is omnipresent too. However, it is only by virtue of his assent and knowledge, and not by virtue of the omnipresence of his body.

We have dealt with two of the ways in which Christ's manhood is present everywhere. First, it is present because of the conjunction of his manhood with his Deity; second, it is present because of the cooperation of his manhood with his Deity. We will now deal with the third manner in which it is present, and that is by the force and efficacy of Christ's sacrifice for the sins of the whole world. We have seen that the body of Christ is a part of that whole nature of man which is united with the Deity of Christ; and it is united with his Deity wherever the Deity is. Therefore, wherever that Deity is, we have an omnipresence of the true conjunction of Christ's bodily presence with Deity. It was the union of the body of Christ with his Deity that made possible the sacrifice for the sins of the whole world; and as this union is omnipresent, it makes the sacrifice omnipresent in force and power throughout all space and through all the generations of men.

Nothing is actually infinite in the world except God; but there is no limit to the value or merit of the sacrificed body of Christ. Every finite number can become infinite by means of addition, and every finite line can become infinite by means of extension. Thus it is with the value of the sacrificed body of Christ, for it has no measured limit in its power of giving us life, but it has an infinite possibility of application.

Suppose we interpret that gracious promise of our Lord and Savior, Jesus Christ, about his presence with us unto the very end of the world, "Lo," he says, "I am with you alway, even unto the end of the world."[6] I see no reason why we cannot explain these words according to what we have said about him as both God and man. He is present with us by the very es-

[6] Mat. 28. 20.

sential Nature of his Deity, and he is present with us as a man because of the assent of his will and understanding to the acts of Deity, and because of the presence of the conjunction and cooperation of his humanity with his Deity. This conjunction and cooperation are as omnipresent as Deity itself.

CHAPTER XIII

Participation in Christ

WE have just dealt with the Person of Christ, and with the omnipresence of Christ; now we will deal with our participation in Christ and Christ's participation in us. Participation is a reciprocal and inward possession by Christ of us, and by us of him, and the possession is by means of a particular sort of having, holding, and inherent conjoining. If we are to understand this mutual participation, we must assume two principles which we have already established. The first principle asserts that every fundamental cause gives something of itself to the things that spring from it; and the second principle asserts that the result is to some extent contained in the cause.

On the basis of these two principles, if the Son of God is "Light of Light,"[1] he must, therefore, be Light that is in Light, for he is "in the bosom of the Father."[2] Owing to the unity of the substance, the Persons of the Godhead must necessarily remain within one another, although they are necessarily distinct from each other. That is because two of them issue from one of them, and one of them from the other two; and of the three of them only one of them is underived.

Again, every parent loves his offspring to that extent to which he himself is to be found in his child. Therefore, the only begotten Son of God must be the only beloved of his Father; and the only begotten Son dwells in the Father because he is eternally generated by his Father, and has his being and life from his Father. And so, the only begotten Son exists in God through an eternal emotion of love.

[1] Nicene Creed.
[2] Jn. 1. 18.

The incarnation of the Son of God causes him, even as man, to dwell in the Father, and the Father in him. Christ, as man, receives life from his Father as the fountain of ever-living Deity, because in the Person of the Word God has joined himself with manhood, and has imparted to manhood a kind of light which has not been given to any other creature beside Christ himself.

Everything that God has made has something of God in it; and God has something of that thing in himself. However, since the substance of God and that of the creature are completely different, the coherence and communion of creature with creature, and of God with creature, are not like the communion of the members of the Trinity, or of Christ with the Father. God influences even the very essence of all things, and without that influence to support them, they would completely disappear, for God has given them their original existence and their continued existence as what they are. Everything, therefore, partakes of God[3]—everything is his offspring, and he influences them all[4].

Everything which God has created is in this sense the offspring of God, and is in him as an effect is in its highest cause; and he is in them, and his assistance and influence are their very life. This is the general indwelling of God in the creature, and the creature in him. There is, however, a special indwelling in man, for among the creatures whom God universally sustains there are some in whom he dwells in a special and distinctive way. If a saving power is added to the general operation of God in the world, it produces a special offspring among men; for by a special and additional generative act some men are born anew. To these new creatures, God gives the gracious and lovable name of sons.[5]

By nature we are the sons of Adam; only by grace and favor

[3] Wis. 7. 23-24.
[4] Heb. 1. 3.
[5] 1 Jn. 3. 1.

are we the sons of God. As by nature we are the sons of Adam, so by a spiritual birth we are the race and progeny, the sons of God's own natural Son. God eternally loves his Son, and since we are the sons of his Son, God must love and prefer us in preference to all others. The children of God dwell in God as their Savior as well as their Creator, because the purpose found in his saving Goodness, his saving Wisdom, and his saving Power, makes him favorably disposed to the children of God.

Even though God, by his foreknowledge, knew whom he would save by his new creative work, and despite the fact that they were eternally in God because he intended to admit them to life; even so, he saves them by his actual adoption of them at a given moment of their lives. In this work of adoption, he is in them as the artisan is in the piece of craftsmanship which he makes. This new life is like all other gifts and benefits that come from God; it comes from the Father, and only from the Father, but by way of the Son, and only by way of the Son, but through the Spirit and only through the Spirit. That is the reason that the Apostle Paul concludes his letter to the Church at Corinth with the wish that the Corinthians might have three gifts, "The grace of the Lord Jesus Christ, and the love of God, and the communion of the Holy Ghost,"* St. Peter summarizes the three gifts as one, the participation in the divine nature.

Therefore, we are in God through Christ, and that eternally, and in accord with God's purpose when he chose us before the world itself was made. It was his everlasting knowledge about us, and his everlasting love of us, which were his reason for choosing us. But although the choice was before all time, we do not really dwell in God until we are actually adopted into the body of his true Church, which is the fellowship of his children.

*2 Cor. 13. 14

His Church is known and loved by him, and that is the reason that those who are in the Church are known to be in him.

The thing that makes us alive is the spirit of the second Adam, and through his body we receive life. That does not mean that his flesh mixes with ours, but it does mean that the union between his body and his Deity, and the cooperation between his body and his Deity, are omnipresent and procure for us our salvation.

It is the union of his Deity with our nature that frees us from the corruption of our nature, and so the condemnation of sin and death, which only has applicability to sinful flesh, has no applicability to him. For that reason, his voluntary death for others prevailed with God and had the force of an expiatory sacrifice. As the Apostle says, the blood of Christ takes away sin because he "through the eternal Spirit offered himself without spot to God."[7] Thus was our human nature made holy and a sacrifice, so that it could take away sin; and thus was it made alive, raised from the grave, and caused to ascend into glory. Because Christ is a spirit who gives life, the highest degree of communion with him is a participation in his spirit, and this participation, St. Cyprian calls "the truest and most intimate communion that can exist between man and that Christ who is both God and man."[8]

No Christian will deny that when Christ sanctified his own flesh by the giving it up to the Holy Ghost, as God, and by receiving the Holy Ghost, as man, he did not do it for himself but for our sakes. Just as a curse came upon all mankind from Adam, so the grace of satisfaction, which was first received by Christ, passed from Christ to the whole race. However, because sin possessed us, his Spirit is prevented from creating these results in us. Therefore, we must participate in the grace and virtue of his body and blood, in order to have the purification

[7] Heb. 9. 14.
[8] Migne, S. L. clxxxix. 1644.

of a new life, and in order to have the future restoration of our bodies. If we do not participate in the grace and virtue of his body and blood, there is no foundation for any other operation of the Spirit of Christ in us, and so it is obvious that Christ imparts himself to us by degrees.

The divine substance of Christ is equally in all of us, and his human substance is equally far away from all of us, and since participation in Christ has many degrees and differences, the participation, therefore, must consist of the effects produced in us by both natures of Christ, and appropriated by us as our very own. If we have these effects within ourselves, we are truly said to possess the One from whom they come, for Christ inhabits our lives and imparts himself to us to the extent that the graces that flow into us from him are more in number and greater in amount.

The Person of Christ is whole, both in the whole Church and in every part of the Church, because he cannot be divided or possessed in degrees. However, participation is more than the presence of Christ's Person, and the mystical unification of his power with the parts and members of his whole Church, for it involves an actual influence of grace upon me. By this influence "I live, yet not I, but Christ liveth in me,"[9] and from him I receive those perfections which will constitute my eternal happiness.

We have seen how the Father is in the Son, and the Son is in the Father; this is the primordial and fundamental form of participation, similar to the mutual participation of the Persons of the Trinity, yet different from it, a participation in which God shares himself with his creatures who are different from him in substance. Both the Father and the Son are in all things, and all things are in them. Next, we have seen what sort of communion Christ has with his Church; we have seen how his Church, and every member of it, participate in him

[9] Gal. 2. 20.

because of a new birth from him. We have seen how he dwells in them through the gift of the Holy Ghost, and through the gift of the vital power of his body and blood. Through these gifts the members of the Church receive by degrees the complete measure of the divine grace that makes us holy and saves us. They are now partakers with Christ in those things that lead us to glory, and they continue to grow until the day of their final exaltation to the state of fellowship with him in glory. However, in this participation in Christ there is no mixture of his flesh with ours, and we do not need any such crude assumption to understand our life in him.

CHAPTER XIV

THE NECESSITY OF THE SACRAMENTS FOR PARTICIPATION IN CHRIST

IT is a stumbling-block to the right understanding of the holy sacraments when their only purpose is made to be that of teaching us by means of the other senses what preaching teaches us through our hearing. The result of such a conception is the easy neglect and careless regard for these heavenly mysteries, and that is to be seen in the lives of those men who hold this opinion most resolutely. Where the word of God can be heard, we can learn its lessons much more directly and more fully through hearing it than we can by observing the sacraments.

Suppose instruction were the only benefit we could reap from the sacraments; then, if we had the opportunity of using the better means of instruction, we would not pay much attention to the worse. The sacraments would in such a case not be esteemed very highly. If they were only means of instruction, it would seem quite superfluous to administer any sacrament to children who are not yet capable of instruction. There must be, therefore, a more excellent and heavenly use of sacraments than that of instruction.

Because of their mixed nature, the sacraments are more debated about and more diversely interpreted than any other aspect of Christianity. The reason for this lies in the fact that a sacrament possesses a great many properties, and as each man notices some special aspect of the same sacrament and disregards the other aspects, the various opinions about the necessity of the sacraments seem to contradict each other. However, these differences of opinion are not as great as it would seem, for if we consider the various duties which every communicant undertakes, we shall find that they are all most necessary.

A consideration of the sacraments reveals many things about them that are necessary. They serve as chains that bind us in obedience to God, as strict obligations that bind us to a mutual exercise of Christian love; they provoke us to godliness; they preserve us from sin; they are memorials of Christ's chief benefits to us. If we consider the time when they were instituted, we see that God has connected them forever with the New Testament, as he previously had connected other rites with the Old Testament. If we consider our weakness, the sacraments are guarantees for the security of our belief; if we compare those who have received them with those who have not received them, we realize that the sacraments mark the difference between those who belong to God and those who are strangers.

In all of these respects, the sacraments are very necessary; but their principal power does not lie in any of these uses, but in the fact that they are heavenly ceremonies, made holy and ordained by God to be administered in his Church. First of all, they are signs of grace given, and they make us realize when God does impart vital and saving grace to all those who are capable of receiving it from him; and, second, they are conditional means required by God of those to whom he does impart grace.

God himself is invisible, and we cannot see him working. Therefore, when in his heavenly wisdom he has some special reason for men to notice his glorious presence, he uses some obvious, sensible sign so that we can know he is operating there, even though we cannot see him. Moses could not see God and live, and yet Moses knew that God was present in an unusual way when he saw the burning bush.[1] Nobody saw the angel by whom God endowed the pool of Bethesda with supernatural power to heal; but the troubling of the waters made the angel's

[1] Ex. 3. 2.

presence known.² The fiery tongues which the Apostles saw told them that the Spirit was upon them although they could not see the Spirit.³

Our situation is similar to that of Moses and the Apostles, because we cannot even understand, to say nothing about see, Christ and his Holy Spirit as they act upon us. Even though we cannot see them, they enter into our souls, and they give us a sign when they come into our lives, and they do so because it pleases Almighty God to communicate to us by sensible means blessings which we cannot otherwise understand.

Grace, therefore, is a result of the sacraments, and is the purpose which the sacraments achieve. It is a benefit which God himself gives to those who receive them; and it comes from God himself and not from any natural or supernatural quality intrinsic to them. Thus, it is clear that the sacraments are necessary, and yet their necessity for supernatural life is not the same kind of necessity as that of food for natural life. Food contains an intrinsic quality necessary for our existence, but the sacraments do not contain in themselves vital force or power. They are not physical, but *moral instruments* of salvation. They are duties of service and worship, and are unprofitable unless they are performed as the Author of grace requires that they should be performed.

The sacraments are sacraments of his grace because they are instruments by which his grace is received. Yet, because they are moral, not physical, instruments, all those who receive the sacraments of his grace do not receive the grace of God. On the other hand, God does not usually wish to bestow the grace of the sacraments on any persons except by the instrumentality of the sacraments. That is true even though the grace received by the instrumentality of the sacraments is received from God himself, and not from the sacraments themselves. Solomon's

²Jn. 5. 4.
³Acts 2. 3.

words of wisdom about the brazen serpent are applicable to the sacraments as well, "He that turned towards it was not healed by the thing he saw, but by thee, O Saviour of all."⁴

The necessity of the sacraments lies in the fact that the saving grace which Christ possesses for the general good of the whole Church he conveys to every member of the Church by means of the sacraments. That is the end, and that is the purpose served by the sacraments as the instruments of God; for although it is we who use them, it is he who makes them effective. He explicitly commands us to use them, and upon the fulfilment of his command the results depend. Therefore, on the one hand, unless we obey his command there seems to be no assurance of these results; and on the other hand, there is no doubt that the sacraments of his grace give what they promise and what they portray, unless they are either not received because of contempt, or received with contempt.

We do not, therefore, consider baptism and the eucharist as bare symbols or memorials of things long past, and we do not consider them bare signs and testimonies which assure us of grace that has been received in times past. Baptism and the eucharist are, in reality, effective means which portray and symbolize that grace by which through reception of these sacraments eternal life is made possible.

Many difficulties about the doctrine of the sacraments have arisen because there has been no distinct explanation of the kind or degree of grace that belongs to each sacrament. Thus, because of this ambiguity, very few people distinctly understand the true reason for the necessity of baptism and the Lord's Supper. It cannot be denied that many of the same results which come to us by the instrumentality of one sacrament may come from the other sacrament also. Even so, baptism only claims that it brings about the beginning of those graces which are completed by mysteries of the eucharist that follow after

⁴Wis. 16. 7. (Great Bible).

baptism. In baptism we receive Jesus Christ once and for all, and we receive him as the one who gives us the beginning of our life; in the eucharist we receive Jesus Christ often, and we receive him as the one who by degrees completes our life.

We receive Jesus Christ by baptism, and we receive from him that saving grace which belongs to baptism; we also receive Jesus Christ by the eucharist, and we receive an impartation of himself through that grace which belongs to the eucharist. As each sacrament has the properties that are common to both, and also a property that is unique to itself, it follows, therefore, that the unique participation in Christ which is the property of one of the sacraments cannot be obtained except from that sacrament of which it is the property.

CHAPTER XV

THE SACRAMENT OF BAPTISM

THE inward grace of the sacraments bears a relationship to the outer form of the sacraments similar to that of the soul and the body. As it is the soul which gives to the body that nature, that quantity, and that shape which are appropriate to the soul, so the inward grace of a sacrament teaches us what outward forms best serve the purpose of that sacrament. The matter of outward form should not be neglected in any part of the Christian religion, and that is particularly true of the sacraments.

Our choice of the outward form depends upon the grace to be conveyed by the sacrament, and the appropriateness of the elements themselves lies in their fitness to the purpose of the sacrament. There is a particular appropriateness in the use of water in baptism, and in the use of bread and wine in the eucharist. Because the grace we receive from the sacraments does not depend upon the natural power of the elements which we see, it is necessary that the words used as a part of the outward form make clear what the sacrament is accomplishing. To do this, we make explicit the meaning of the sacrament by words taken from the mouth of our Lord himself when he instituted the sacrament, and by these words we are clearly told what is really accomplished through the visible elements.

When we describe the blessed sacraments, we usually use the same term to denote both the outward and visible elements, and the secret grace which these elements signify. That is the reason that it is usual in definitions of the sacraments to make grace their reality, and the elements the visible signs of that grace. The relationship between the grace of the sacrament and the elements of the sacrament is similar to that between the soul and the body.

Suppose in our definition of a sacrament we separate that which is secret from that which is visible. This distinction is necessary if we are to distinguish between the sacramental grace and sacrament. If we make this distinction, the term sacrament applies only to the outward and visible elements, and not to grace conveyed by the sacrament. If we now analyze the sacrament as an outward and visible sign, we discover that it has two phases, (1) the elements which are signs of the grace conveyed, and (2) the words which tell us what is accomplished by the instrumentality of the elements. Thus, if our analysis begins with a separation of the sacrament into outward sign and inward grace, and then continues with an analysis of the outward sign into the elements used and the words said, the sacrament consists of three things, (1) the inward secret grace, (2) the elements, and (3) the words indicating the meaning of the elements.

These three things are essential to baptism; but there are other things involved which are not indicated by the definition, and are only implied and presupposed by it. One of these presuppositions is the serious intent of the Church in ordering the observance of the sacraments, for they are religious and mystical acts, and they do not have this character unless they are celebrated by the Church with serious intention. We cannot know what is in a minister's mind when he administers a sacrament, and we are not obliged to know, for we assume that he has the intention of the Church in regard to the sacraments when he acts as the minister of the Church.

We have seen that a sacrament consists of the inward secret grace, the elements used, and the words of institution. These three things, and the serious intention of the Church in ordering the observance of the sacrament, make it valid. We shall see that all other additions, however useful and desirable, must be held accessories that can be dispensed with in case of necessity. In baptism, the orders, the ceremonies, the prayers, the lessons, the sermons, the actions, and all the other additions, are only accessory features of the outward and visible sign. They are accessory aspects which the wisdom of the Church of Christ arranges to carry out the central meaning of the sacrament in a more explicit form.

Again, such accessories are made for the sacrament, and the sacrament is not made for them. They adorn and do not constitute the sacrament, and therefore the sacrament does not depend upon them. They are not the essential factors in baptism, and baptism is far more necessary than any such incidental rites or ceremonies for the better administration of baptism. Even though the situation should not allow us to use all the ceremonial accessories, it would be better to have baptism without them than it would be to wait for a ceremonially correct baptism and find that the opportunity for all baptism has been lost. If we accept these premises, it is a valid inference that in those cases of necessity which will not allow a delay until baptism be administered with the usual ceremonial, we may administer baptism without it. It is better to do that than to allow any man to die without baptism.

A few statements will make clear the kind of necessity involved in baptism. First, we must understand what is meant by necessity, and then we must see in what sense baptism is necessary. Those things are called necessary which are either the source of some great good or the means of avoiding some grievous evil. If regeneration were not in this sense necessary for eternal life, would Christ have said to Nicodemus, "Except a man be born again, he cannot see the kingdom of God"?[1] Christ's next words are, "Except a man be born of water and of the Spirit, he cannot enter into the kingdom of God."[2] By

---

[1] Jn. 3. 3.
[2] Jn. 3. 5.

these words he shows us that the Spirit is as necessary for regeneration as regeneration is necessary for eternal life.

These words also prove to us that just as the Spirit is the inward cause of our regeneration, so water is the outward means of our regeneration. If baptism by water were not in some sense necessary, why is our new birth spoken of as "of water" as well as "of the Spirit"?[3] Why is it that we are taught that God sanctifies and cleanses his Church ."with the washing of water by the word"?[4] Why does one Apostle of Christ call baptism "the washing of regeneration"[5] and another advise men to receive outward baptism "in the name of Jesus Christ for the remission of sins"?[6]

There is a kind of necessity about baptism, but it is not an absolute necessity. That would only be true if baptism were a condition without which regeneration could not come to be. In that case baptism would have such natural or supernatural power in itself that regeneration would not take place without it, and then nobody would ever receive grace before baptism. If you do not first have the cause, you do not have the results that necessarily spring from it. Thus, if baptism were absolutely necessary for the reception of grace, no man would receive grace without it. In many cases we know that this is not so, but in other cases, although we do not make baptism the necessary cause of grace, yet we do recognize that grace given in baptism has a kind of dependence on the outward sacrament. God wishes us to use the outward sacrament not only as a sign or token of what we receive, but also as an instrument or means by which we receive grace. Baptism is a sacrament instituted by God in his Church as a means of incorporating us into Christ; and thus by his most precious merit we obtain that grace which takes away all former guiltiness, and that divine virtue of the Holy Spirit which gives to the powers of the soul their first inclination to a future newness of life.

[3] Ibid.
[4] Eph. 5. 26.
[5] Tit. 3. 5.
[6] Acts 2. 38.

CHAPTER XVI

THE SACRAMENT OF THE BODY AND BLOOD OF CHRIST

THE grace which we receive by means of the holy eucharist does not begin life, but continues it. Therefore, no one receives this sacrament before baptism because nothing dead can take nourishment. The thing that grows must be alive in order to grow, and if our bodies did not constantly waste away it would not be necessary to have food to restore them. Perhaps the grace of baptism would be sufficient for our eternal life if our spiritual being were not impaired each day after our baptism. In the life to come, where neither body nor soul can decay, our souls will require this sacrament as little as our bodies will require physical nourishment. However, as long as the days of our warfare shall last, and as long as we are subject to decay and growth in grace, the words of our Lord and Savior, Jesus Christ, will remain true, "Except ye eat the flesh of the Son of Man, and drink his blood, ye have no life in you."[1]

Life is the true end for man, and those who have received a new life through baptism are told what kind of food is necessary to continue that new life. Those who wish to live the life of God must eat the flesh and drink the blood of the Son of Man, because his flesh and blood are a part of the diet which we must have in order to live. In infancy we are incorporated into Christ by baptism, and receive the grace of his Spirit, and we receive it without knowing that we are receiving it; but in the eucharist the gift is received in another way, because we know by grace what the grace is which God gives us. We see the stages of our growth in holiness and virtue, and we recognize their existence; and we know that the strength of our life

[1] Jn. 6. 53.

begun in Christ is Christ. We realize that his flesh is meat and his blood is drink; and these things we do not merely imagine, but we really know. They are so truly known that by faith we taste of eternal life when we receive the body and blood given to us in the sacrament. The grace of the sacrament is recognized as the food which we eat and drink.

Just after the feeding of the five thousand on the Sea of Tiberius,[2] the Disciples learned from Christ that his flesh and blood were the true source of eternal life, not because of the bare force of their own substance, but because of the dignity and worth of the Person who offered them and still offers them up as a sacrifice for the whole world. The Disciples also learned that the body and blood were a life for each particular man only by being received by him himself as an individual. They understood this much although they did not yet perfectly understand what was the consequence of such a doctrine, and they did not understand until they gathered together for no other reason which they could imagine except to eat that Passover which Moses had instituted.

Then, they saw their Lord and Master take the chosen elements of bread and wine in his hands, and, with eyes lifted to heaven, consecrate and bless them for the endless good of all generations till the world's end. Thus, by virtue of his divine benediction, these elements were made forever the instruments of life, and thus the Disciples were the first who were commanded to receive them, and the first who were promised, if they duly administered them, that the bread and the wine would be the channels of life and the vehicles by which his body and blood would be brought to them, and this was a promise not only to them but to their successors.

All of this had happened, and they had heard him say, "Take, eat; this is my body; drink ye all of it; for this is my blood."[3] Could they have done what he had told them to do, believed

[2] Jn. 6. 25 ff.
[3] Mat. 26. 26-28.

what he had promised, and experienced the results he had promised, and not have been filled with a kind of fearful admiration for that heaven which they saw within themselves? We are taught by their joy and comfort that this heavenly food is given for the satisfaction of our empty souls, and not for the exercise of our investigating and overly subtle minds.

If we have any doubt as to what is expressed by these admirable words, let that one be our teacher as to the meaning of Christ, to whom Christ himself was a schoolmaster. Let our Lord's Apostle be his interpreter, and let us content ourselves with his explanation, "The cup of blessing which we bless, is it not the communion of the blood of Christ? The bread which we break, is it not the communion of the body of Christ?"[4] Is there anything clearer and easier than the fact that just as Christ is called our life because we obtained life through him, so the parts of this sacrament are called his body and blood because when we receive these elements we do receive the body and blood of Christ?

We say that the bread and the wine are his body and his blood because through their instrumentality we participate in his body and blood, and that is a valid assertion because we quite properly give the name of the effect to the cause which produces it, for the cause is in the result which grows out of that cause. Our souls and bodies receive eternal life, and this life in them has as its source and cause the Person of Christ, and his body and blood are the source from which this life flows. The influence of the heavens is in plants, animals and men, and in everything which they make alive; but the body and blood of Christ are in that communicant to which they minister in a far more divine and mystical kind of union, a union which makes us one with him, even as he and the Father are one.

The real presence of Christ's most blessed body and blood should not be sought for in the sacrament, but in the worthy

[4] 1 Cor. 10. 16.

receiver of it. The very order of our Savior's words agrees with this interpretation of the meaning of the sacrament. First, he says, "Take, eat;" and only after that does he say, "This is my body." First, he says, "Drink ye all of it;" and only after that does he say, "This is my blood of the new testament, which is shed for many for the remission of sins."[5] It was only after the eating that the bread became the body of Christ; it was only after the drinking that the wine became his blood. The only interpretation that seems appropriate to these words of Christ is that which says that the bread is his body, and the cup is his blood only in the very heart and soul of the receiver, and that the sacramental elements themselves really exhibit, but do not really contain in themselves, that grace which it has pleased God to give us by means of them.

Everybody confesses that the grace of baptism is poured into the soul of man, and that although we receive it by means of water, it is neither located in the water, nor is the water changed into it. Why, then, should men think that the grace of the eucharist must be in the elements before that grace is in us who receive the sacrament?

The fruit of the eucharist is participation in the body and blood of Christ. There is not a single sentence in Holy Scripture that says we cannot be made partakers of his body and blood by means of this sacrament, unless the body and blood are contained in the elements or the elements converted in them. Christ's words about his body and his blood are words of promise, for when he says, "This is my body," and "This is my blood,"[6] he promises us his body and his blood.

We all agree that Christ really and truly carries out his promise by means of the sacrament; but why do we trouble ourselves by such fierce contests about consubstantiation and the question whether the elements themselves contain Christ or

[5] Mat. 26. 26-27.
[6] Mat. 26. 26-27.

not? Even if consubstantiation or transubstantiation are true, it does not benefit us, and if they are not true it does not handicap us. Our participation in Christ through the sacraments depends upon the cooperation of his omnipotent power, and that power makes the sacrament a means of creating his body and blood in us. Whether there is or is not such a change in the elements themselves, as some people imagine, need not make any great difference to us.

Let us, then, accept that in which we all agree, and then consider why the rest should not be considered superfluous rather than urged as necessary. In the first place, it is generally agreed that this sacrament is a real participation in Christ, and that by its means he imparts his full Person as the mystical head of every soul who receives him and thereby becomes a very member incorporate in his mystical body, which is the blessed company of all faithful people.

In the second place, it is also agreed that the communicant who receives the Person of Christ through the sacrament also receives the Holy Spirit who sanctifies the communicant as it sanctified Christ who is the head of all those who participate in him. In the third place, it is commonly held that whatever power or virtue there is in Christ's sacrificed body and blood we freely and fully receive by this sacrament. In the fourth place, it is agreed that the result of the sacrament is a real transmutation of our souls and bodies from sin to righteousness, from death and corruption to immortality and life. In the fifth place, all believe that the sacramental elements are only corruptible and earthly things; therefore, they must seem to be an unlikely instrument to work out such admirable effects in man. For that reason, we must not rest our confidence in these elements themselves, but put our trust altogether in the strength of his glorious power, which he can and will give us. Through these his gifts and creatures of bread and wine, he will give that which he has promised to give us.

PART THREE

THE ORDERS OF THE MINISTRY

CHAPTER XVII. The Church Mystical and the Church Visible
CHAPTER XVIII. The Church, the Ministry, and Temporal Happiness
CHAPTER XIX. The Ministry of Things Divine
CHAPTER XX. The Three Degrees of Ecclesiastical Order in the Ministry
CHAPTER XXI. Bishops in the Church of Christ

CHAPTER XVII

THE CHURCH MYSTICAL AND THE CHURCH VISIBLE

THAT Church of Christ which is appropriately called his mystical body is one and only one; and no man is aware of it through his senses. No one can see this Church because one part of it is in heaven and is already with Christ, and the other part is on earth. Although the natural persons who make up the earthly part of the mystical body of Christ are visible, we do not see them as members of this Church, and so we have no way of knowing whether they are truly members of his body or not. We cannot perceive such a body by our senses, and we can only grasp it by the intellectual concepts of our minds. By such an intellectual process we know that this body is a real and collective body which contains within itself a great number of individuals. We know it is a mystical body because the mystery of the union of so many people in Christ's body is completely foreign to the visible.

When we read in the Scripture about the endless love and saving grace shown by God to his Church, the Church spoken of is the mystical Church of Christ. When our Lord and Savior said of that Church which he calls his sheep, "And I give unto them eternal life; and they shall never perish, neither shall any man pluck them out of my hand,"[1] he is speaking of the mystical Church. Those who are members of this society are distinguished from those who are not by clues which are invisible to our senses but are visible to God and to God alone, who sees their hearts and understands all their secret thoughts, and who clearly discerns who they are.

Everybody knew that Nathanael was an Israelite; but our Savior, who saw more deeply and testified with more certainty

[1] Jn. 10. 28.

than men, said, "Behold an Israelite indeed, in whom is no guile!"[2] Suppose we assert, as Peter did, that we love the Lord, and assert it publicly. Kindness makes people tend to believe everything, and therefore kind people are likely to think that we do really love the Lord, and they will believe that so long as there is no proof to the contrary. But who can say that our love is sincere, and that it comes from "a pure heart, and of a good conscience, and of faith unfeigned"?[3] Who can say that except the Searcher of all men's hearts, the one who alone intuitively knows who are his own?

The everlasting promise of love, mercy, and blessedness belong to the mystical Church; but the duties which obligate the Church of God are duties which belong to the group which we can see. This visible Church, like the mystical Church, is one, and has existed since the beginning of the world, and will continue to the world's end. It is composed of two parts, the one that existed before the coming of Christ, the other that has existed since his coming. The part which has existed since the coming of Christ is composed of those who either have or shall have embraced the Christian religion; and its appropriate name is the Church of Christ.

Like the invisible Church, the visible Church of Christ is one body, and that is the reason the Apostle says quite plainly of all of us who are Christian people, that "whether we be Jews or Gentiles, whether we be bond or free," "we are all baptized into one body," and "members of that one body."[4] There is a unity in that visible body of which the Church of Christ consists, and the unity is that of the common life of the body of Christ, a life shared by all who are parts of his body. They are "members of that one body"[5] because they all profess themselves to be servants of one Lord, because they have one faith

[2] Jn. 1. 47.
[3] 1 Tim. 1. 5.
[4] 1 Cor. 12. 12-13.
[5] Ibid.

which they all acknowledge, and because they are baptized with one baptism by which they are all initiated. "There is one body, and one Spirit, even as ye are called in one hope of your calling; one Lord, one faith, one baptism."[6]

Therefore, the visible Church of Jesus Christ is one, and it is one in the external profession of those things which supernaturally belong to the very essence of Christianity and are by necessity required of each Christian man. "Let all the house of Israel know assuredly, that God hath made that same Jesus, whom ye have crucified, both Lord and Christ."[7] Therefore, no one is a Christian who does not call him Master and Lord. That is the reason that first at Antioch and afterwards everywhere, all members of the visible Church were called Christians even by the heathen. The Christians considered the name precious and glorious, but the rest of the world thought that even Jesus Christ himself was detestable. If Jesus Christ was detestable, so were all those who considered him to be their Lord. He foresaw that this would be so, and he forearmed his Church so that it might bear this disdain without discomfort. "All these things will they do unto you for my name's sake."[8] "Yea, the time cometh, that whosoever killeth you will think that he doeth God service."[9] "These things have I told you, that when the time shall come, ye may remember that I told you of them."[10]

However, the fact that we call Jesus Christ Lord is not enough to prove that we are Christians, unless we also embrace that faith which Christ proclaimed to the world. To prove that the angel of Pergamus remained Christian, the Spirit of Christ said, "Thou holdest fast my name, and hast not denied my faith."[11] As to the faith of Christ, Tertullian says that "its

[6] Eph. 4. 4-5.
[7] Acts 2. 36.
[8] Jn. 15. 21.
[9] Jn. 16. 2.
[10] Jn. 16. 4.
[11] Rev. 2. 13.

rule is only one, is unchangeable, and cannot be reframed in a better form than that in which it now exists."[12] He shows us what that rule of faith is by repeating those few articles that make up the Christian belief.

Before Tertullian's time, Irenaeus said, "Even though the Church is scattered throughout the whole world and to the very ends of the earth, it has received its belief from the Apostles and their disciples." He recited the articles of his belief, and the substance of his creed is the same as that of Tertullian. Then he says, "Even though the Church is spread out far and wide, she preserves this faith as if it were contained in one house, as if she herself had but one soul, one heart, and no more. She proclaims, teaches, and gives the faith to her members in a uniform manner, as if God had given the Church only one tongue with which to speak. The most eloquent leader of the Church asserts no more than this faith, and the least wise does not utter less than this in the profession of his faith."[13]

Suppose we know the Christian faith and accept it; even so, this is only an approach to the visible Church, for we do not enter into it except by the door of baptism. Directly after his confession of the Christian faith, the Eunuch was baptized by Philip, directly after his confession Paul was baptized by Ananias, and directly after their confession a huge crowd of three thousand people were baptized by Peter. When they were once baptized they were then counted among those who were joined to the visible Church.

When we describe the unique characteristics of Christians, we do not mention those virtues that are a matter of moral righteousness and uprightness of life, because they are not the characteristics of men as Christians but of men as men. It is true, of course, that the absence of these virtues excludes us from salvation. So does the absence of inner belief; so does despair

---
[12]Tertull., *de virgin.* c. 1.
[13]Iren., *advers haeres.* lib. 1. cap. 2 & 3.

or lack of hope; so does the lack of Christian love and charity. We are speaking, however, at this point, not of the mystical Church, whose members are known only to God, but of the visible Church, whose children are signed with the mark of "one Lord, one faith, one baptism." Where there is one Lord acknowledged, one faith confessed, one baptism received by any, the Church acknowledges them to be her children. The only ones she considers aliens and strangers are those who do not share in "one Lord, one faith, one baptism."[14]

Saracens, Jews, and infidels are excluded from the Church because they do not share in one Lord, and faith and baptism. We cannot exclude any one from the visible Church as long as he has them. It is clear that all men must be either Christian or not Christian; and if they outwardly profess to be Christians, then they are part of the visible Church of Christ. All are Christians by outward profession if they profess one Lord and one faith in one baptism; and that is true even though they are impious idolaters, wicked heretics, persons who should be excommunicated and even those who should have been cast out because of their notorious perverseness. We do not deny that these idolaters and other such wicked people are imps and members of Satan as long as they continue to be wicked, yet, because of their profession, they are members of the visible Church of Christ.

Can it be possible that the same man should belong both to the Synagogue of Satan and to the Church of Jesus Christ? It is, of course, not possible to belong to the Synagogue of Satan and to that Church which is Christ's mystical body, because his mystical body is made up only of true Israelites, true sons of Abraham, true servants and saints of God. However, it is quite possible, and oftentimes is true, that the same man can belong to both the Synagogue of Satan and the visible Church of Jesus Christ. There are members of the visible

[14] Eph. 4. 5.

body and Church of Jesus Christ, members because of the principal articles of their outward profession, who, because of their inward disposition of mind, their external conversation, and even some articles of their very profession, deserve both the hate of God himself and that of the sounder parts of the visible Church.

Therefore, our Savior compares the Kingdom of Heaven with a net "that was cast into the sea, and gathered of every kind."[15] He compares his Church with a field where the tares were seen to grow in the midst of the good wheat,[16] and the tares were allowed to grow together with the wheat until the final consummation of the world. God has always had a visible Church on earth, and he always will. At one time the people of God worshipped the golden calf in the wilderness; at another time they did reverence to the brazen serpent; at still another time they served the gods of the nations. Sometimes they bowed their knees to Baal; sometimes they burnt incense and offered sacrifices to idols.

On these occasions the wrath of God flamed up against them and their prophets most justly condemned them as an adulterous and wicked generation. The prophets told them they had forsaken the living God, and that God no longer would show them that special mercy that made them his faithful children. Even so, in the very depths of their disobedience and rebellion, they continued to be the sheep of his visible flock as long as they possessed the law and the seal of his covenant.

God, therefore, always has had a Church composed of his visible flock; and not only did he have a Church among the thousands who never bowed their knees to Baal, but also among those whose knees were bowed to Baal, for they also were a part of the visible Church of God. In his complaint,

[15]Mat. 13. 47.
[16]Mat. 13. 24 ff.

the Prophet Elijah did not mean to say that the Church had been wholly extinguished. What he meant was that he was the only one who was left who had a true and upright heart towards God, and who wished to serve God according to God's holy will.

CHAPTER XVIII

The Church, the Ministry, and Temporal Happiness

WE now come to the consideration of the public ministry of holy things according to the laws of the Christian religion. The ministry is a matter of action, and action is understood through the object with which it deals and the purpose at which it aims. In the case of the Church, the object with which it deals is both God and man. Its object is God because he is publicly worshipped by his Church; and its object is men because they can become happy by means of Christian discipline. Thus, the whole aim of the Church is the honor of God and the salvation of man.

Whether we consider men as individuals or as gathered together into groups or bodies, we know that every man's religion is the well-spring of other healthy, genuine virtues. We know that men's full joy and happiness spring from religion, and that is true in part for this world and completely for the world to come, because, while they live they are blessed of God, and when they die their works follow after them. For this reason we must realize that the very earthly peace and prosperity, secular happiness, and the temporal and natural good fortune of both men and nations are chiefly dependent upon religion. All of this clearly proves that the priest is a pillar of that commonwealth in which he faithfully serves God.

Among earthly blessings the lowest in the scale is wealth; the highest is reputation. That is the reason we consider the winning of honor an ample recompense for the loss of any other natural benefit. However, as there is no certainty of the continuity of worldly benefits, nature has taught us to value them not for their own sake but for the sake of something that is absolutely good, such as the exercise of virtue and the knowledge of theoretic truth. No one whose desires are as they ought to be would wish to live, breathe, or move without doing that which is befitting a man to do.

If, therefore, we could not do things suited to human living, we would grow weary of even life itself. We value health, because sickness produces the pain that incapacitates us for action. Again, we delight in a large number of friends because our life is made up of many activities, and many helping hands are needed to assist us to promote them.

Also, we would not think that there was any difference between a bad day and a good day, if the bad day did not hinder our action and the good day did not add to the freedom of our action. If we succeed in what we are trying to do, we are pleased, and not so much because of the benefit we derive from our actions as from the proof that our actions have been skillfully done. Riches, likewise, are not an end in themselves, but are valued for something beyond themselves, for if a man has them and does nothing with them they are a reproach. Again, honor is usually considered not an end in itself but an indication of more than usual virtue and merit. That is the reason ambitious minds desire honor; and their endeavors are a proof of how much nature has as its purpose the attaining of those virtues which honor usually indicates.

Thus health, friendship, riches and honor are all relative, and point to values beyond themselves. Even though action itself is relative, we take so much pleasure in it that we desire that the work which we love may go on although we ourselves have departed this life. That is the reason we hand over to others the means we have accumulated to work out our purpose, and we plan the best we can to make these activities perpetual. Thus, our action itself is not an end in itself.

It seems, therefore, that all forms of temporal happiness are relative, and none are good in an absolute sense. They are good in relation to that absolute good to which they are instrumental; and hence, they cannot absolutely and in themselves fulfill our sound desires. Some stupid people have the crude and depraved idea that only the people with the fullest stomachs are the happiest. The greatest happiness they wish for the commonwealth in which they live is to be found in the fact of its prosperity and its continued existence, in the fact that extravagant people will be forced to spend without limit, in the fact that the poor may sleep and the rich feed them; and they desire that nothing unpleasant will be commanded and that no one will be told not to do anything he wants to do.

They desire that kings will make the lives of their subjects easy, and not question too much about their conduct; they desire that wantonness, excess, and lasciviousness of life be allowed, and that no misdemeanor be punished except the dislike of a condition which is as satisfactory as this would be. Far be it for the just to dwell either in or near the tents of such wretched pleasures.

We affirm that religion and the fear of God are as productive of secular prosperity as they are of the everlasting bliss of the world to come. Otherwise, godliness could not be said to fulfill the promises of both this life and the life to come, and so adequately fulfill them that David could say that he had "not seen the righteous forsaken."[1]

We admit that religion produces secular prosperity, but we must understand that this general proposition is subject to certain special limitations. First of all, we must never forget that certain insane and diseased minds are most benefited when they do not have the very things which are beneficial to others. Our heavenly Physician must judge in these cases; but in other cases, noted by the wise man, God shortens men's lives lest wickedness should change their understanding.

Also, we should remember that the measure of our prosperity is relative and is proportional to the needs of our present life.

[1] Ps. 37. 25.

External goods are instruments of action, and good workmen want tools suited to their work, rather than ones pleasing to the eye. A servant does not need many of the things necessary for a professional man, and the man of inferior position does not need many of those necessary for a person of higher rank. Surely it is obvious that a man is blessed with worldly goods if he has those which are necessary for the performance of the duties which his station and position require.

Because of human folly, and the tendency to become puffed up, too high a flow of good fortune is dangerous; and because of the reality of human impatience and because of the fact that necessity is usually stronger than human virtue, too low an ebb of prosperity is quite as dangerous. We know Solomon's wise and moderate desire, "Give me neither poverty nor riches."⁷ Those who belong to either extreme—the over-honored, the over-strong, the over-noble, or the over-wealthy; or on the opposite end, the over-poor, the over-weak, or the utterly ignoble, —find it hard to listen to reason. The first group tends to violence and serious crime; the second group tends to petty offences. For the great like to exhibit their strength, and the weak like to help themselves by malicious cleverness. When we take everything into consideration, we realize that even for kings and princes moderation is the safest and happiest condition, and we know that moderation lies between too much and too little bread.

Again, we ought not to expect continuous prosperity even in the case of those who are considered happy. Neither should we expect the course either of men's lives or of public affairs to be drawn out in an even thread, because the nature of things will not allow that. What we should do is make an impartial survey and discover what all the factors really are; and then we should realize that just as we consider a man good whose virtues are great and whose faults are moderate, so we should con-

⁷Prov. 30. 8.

sider a man fortunate, or a state happy, who has flourished, and has not later experienced so tragic a change as to become an object of pity to others.

We must remember that the truest happiness consists in the highest operation of the nobler part of man, and that this part sometimes exhibits its highest perfection by enduring what nature endures with most difficulty rather than by enjoying those benefits which please nature most. Therefore, that temporal happiness which accompanies religion should not be considered impaired if we lose one good and purchase a better, or if we suffer misery for a greater praise and honor.

However, this is a matter of degree, since we must decide by an accurate measurement how much a given man should sacrifice for a greater good if he is to be happy. The exception to this is those heroic saints whose sufferings actually make them glorious. In a word, when we call a man happy we do not mean that he has had no misfortunes, but we do mean that he has such a sound mind that neither misery nor prosperity can disturb him.

The fortunate man may have miseries, but if the distressing events which happened to him are not the result of his wickedness and do not seem in the eyes of impartial judges to have resulted from divine revenge, the unfortunate events are counted up as a part of those human accidents to which we are all subject. No misery is to be considered other than usual or human if God allows us to pass through it and come safe to the shore, just as no days of prosperity are considered happy if they end in tears.

Without the help of a spiritual ministry, religion cannot plant itself, for the fruits of religion do not appear automatically. This assertion needs no further proof; but if it did need it, I would declare that all things that come from God are joined together by wonderful art and wisdom with the glue of mutual assistance. In the hierarchy of relations, the lowest in the series receive from the ones nearest them that influence which comes from the highest.

That is the organization of all reality, and therefore, since the Church is the most absolute of all the works of God, it is organized with the same harmony as that of nature; and in his work of grace, as in his works of nature, he works his will by hands and instruments which are subordinate to the power of his own spirit. Man does not like to feel any obligation to any one but himself, and such subordination helps produce a salutory humility, and also nourishes that divine affection which makes us love each other not as men but as angels of God.

Ministerial actions which lead immediately to God's honor and man's happiness are either contemplative or active. If they are contemplative they help the principal work of the ministry; if they are administrative, they consist in conducting the services in the house of God, and in giving men those supreme medicines of grace of which we have already spoken. So it seems that we owe the guides of our souls as much as our souls are worth, even though the debt of our temporal blessings should be cancelled.

CHAPTER XIX

THE MINISTRY OF THINGS DIVINE

AS God himself instituted the office of the ministry of things divine, a man may not undertake it unless he does so by legal power and authority. God never fails to furnish man with the necessities of human life, and that is the reason he has given us the light of his heavenly truth, for if we did not have it we would have to wander in the darkness, and that would mean endless perdition and woe.

Because of his abundant mercy God has provided certain men who are to take care of the execution of the offices which God has provided for the good of the whole world. These men have their authority from him, and they have it whether God gives it to them directly or whether they receive it indirectly from the Church in his name. The reason for this is that it is inappropriate for every sort of man whatsoever to undertake an office of such great importance.

The ministers of God are not ministers simply because they are subordinated to God, for princes and civil magistrates are also subordinated to God. These civil authorities are under the supreme hand of divine Providence because God sustains them when they carry out judgment and justice; but the ministers of God have their authority from God, and not from men. They are Christ's ambassadors and laborers, he alone gives them their commission because they manage his private affairs. God is the Father of spirits; and Jesus Christ is the purchaser of our souls; and the ministry of Christ is concerned with God's relationship to our spirits and Christ's redemption of our souls.

The commission of the ministry is from Jesus Christ himself. No angel in heaven could have given such a commission as our Lord gave to Peter, "Feed my sheep; preach; baptize: do this in rememberance of me; whose soever sins ye remit, they are remitted unto them, and whose soever sins ye retain, they are retained." These are not terrestial words, but are words uttered from the clouds above.

The power of the ministry of God brings men from darkness to glory, it raises men from the earth and brings God himself down from heaven. The ministry blesses the visible elements, and every day it produces invisible grace through them, and thus gives us the Holy Ghost. The ministry administers that flesh which was given for the life of the world, and that blood which was poured out for the redemption of our souls, and when it pours curses upon the heads of the wicked they perish, and when it revokes that curse they live again. O wretched blindness, if we do not admire such great power, and more wretched if we understand the ministry and even so imagine that anyone but God could have bestowed such power!

Christ has imparted power to his ministry both over that mystical body which is the society of souls, and over that natural body of the eucharist in which Christ by the gift of himself unites the natural and the supernatural into one. The ministry of the eucharist was called by the ancients "the making of Christ's body."[1]

The power of the ministry is called a mark, and is indelible because it distinguishes the clergy from other men and makes them a special order consecrated to the service of the Most High and concerned with things with which other people may not meddle. The clergy are different from other men, and that difference makes them a distinct order, as Tertullian tells us. St. Paul himself divides the Church of Christ into two parts.[2] One of these parts is called by him the unlearned, and that part we call today the order of the laity; the other part we name today the order of the clergy. The spiritual power which God

[1] Migne, S. L. xxii. 352.
[2] 1 Cor. 14. 16-24.

has given the clergy is the power of their order, and that power consists in the execution of those holy things which are called "things pertaining to God."[3]

We must now consider the memorable words of our Lord and Savior which we use in the giving of orders to the clergy. They are, "Receive the Holy Ghost."[4] The expression "Holy Ghost" is used to indicate not only the Person but the gifts of the Holy Ghost, and we know that spiritual gifts are not only the ability to do such miraculous things as speaking languages which were never taught us, curing diseases without medicine, and the like, but the very authority and power which are given to men in the Church to be ministers of holy things.

These powers of the ministry belong to the number of gifts of which the Holy Ghost is the author. Therefore, the one who ordains and delegates this power may say without absurdity, "Receive the Holy Ghost."[5] The reception of the Holy Ghost means the reception of the kind of power which the Spirit of Christ has given to the Church. It is the kind of power which neither prince nor potentate, neither king nor Caesar, but only the Church can give.

Our Lord and Savior, after his resurrection from the dead, gave the Apostles their commission. He said, "All power is given unto me in heaven and in earth. Go ye therefore, and teach all nations, baptizing them in the name of the Father, and of the Son, and of the Holy Ghost: teaching them to observe all things whatsoever I have commanded you."[6] He puts it briefly when he says, "As my Father hath sent me, even so send I you."[7] St. John says that immediately after these words "he breathed on them, and saith unto them, Receive ye the Holy Ghost."[8] He most probably meant by these words that

[3] Heb. 2. 17.
[4] Jn. 20. 22. (Ordinal vers.)
[5] Ibid.
[6] Mat. 28. 18-20.
[7] Jn. 20. 21.
[8] Jn. 20. 22.

he was giving to them a gift at that very time, for he said to them, "Receive," and he indicated that he was giving it to them by breathing upon them.

Our task, then, is to determine what grace he was giving his Apostles when he said, "Receive the Holy Ghost." The Apostles certainly did not receive miraculous power at that time, for that promise was to be fulfilled afterwards. St. Luke makes this clear, for he indicates that the promise of miraculous powers was to be fulfilled at a future time. "And, behold, I send the promise of my Father upon you: but tarry ye in the city of Jerusalem, until ye be endued with power from on high."[9] Therefore, when he said, "Receive," he did not mean a promise of power to be bestowed later, but some other gift of the Spirit, the gift of the Holy Ghost in another form, and one which was then given to them by our Savior.

The gift of the Holy Ghost which he then gave to them was a holy and spiritual authority, an authority over the souls of men, an authority which was in part the power to remit and to retain sin. He makes this so clear by his next words that he seems to wish to remove every possible misconstruction of language, "Receive ye the Holy Ghost: whose soever sins ye remit, they are remitted unto them; and whose soever sins ye retain, they are retained."[10]

The first three evangelists tell us that before his passion Christ promised his Disciples the gift of the keys of the kingdom of heaven, and that after his resurrection he promised them the miraculous power of the Holy Ghost. St. John makes clear the meaning of the promise of the keys, for there was a special gift of the Holy Ghost before the gift of miraculous power that came after his ascension. Christ invested his Apostles with the power of the Holy Ghost for the remitting and retaining of sin.

The power and authority delivered to the ordinand by means

[9] Lk. 24. 49.
[10] Jn. 20. 22-23.

of these words are a gift, a gracious gift which the Spirit of God bestows. But besides that, we know that the hand of the bishop which lays upon us the function of our ministry does, by the very words, assure the ordinand, when he receives the "burden of the people,"[11] that he will have the presence of the Spirit with him as his assistance, aid, and support in whatever he does in the faithful discharge of his duty.

We know, therefore, that when we take orders we receive the presence of the Holy Ghost as our guide, director, and strengthener in our ways, and also as the authority for those actions which belong to our work and calling. Can our ears hear such words in the solemnity of the office of ordination, or can we at any time remember them and seriously think about them without much admiration and joy? If we remove from the ministry what these words imply, there is nothing left in the ministry of God in which to glory.

The gift of the Holy Ghost, which was given by our Savior in his first ordinations, is also given to those who have entered the vocation of the ministry throughout the ages, and is given in no less degree than it was when God gave his Spirit through Moses to those who assisted Moses in the government of Israel. The Lord said to Moses, "And I will come down and talk with thee there: and I will take of the spirit which is upon thee, and put it upon them; and they shall bear the burden of the people with thee, that thou bear it not thyself alone."[12] This authority passed from those whom Moses commissioned to their successors.

And so it is with us in our ministry, for even our most trivial and meanest duties are performed with such a virtue of power that it dignifies, graces, and authorizes our acts in a way that they cannot be challenged by any other offices on earth. We preach, we pray, we baptize, we communicate, we condemn, we absolve, we perform other ministerial acts. When we do so,

[11] Num. 11. 17.
[12] Num. 11. 17.

we dispense God's mysteries, and our words, judgments, acts, and deeds are not ours, but are those of the Holy Ghost.

It is enough if we believe this without dissimulation and with our whole heart. It is enough to banish whatever may be rightly thought to be corrupt in the bestowing, using, or in even considering our ministerial powers otherwise than we should. We abhor every word and action that bestows the gifts of the Holy Ghost profanely, that uses them carelessly, and degradedly values them.

CHAPTER XX

THE THREE DEGREES OF ECCLESIASTICAL ORDER IN THE MINISTRY

LET us deal with the ministry of the Gospel of Jesus Christ. Just as the whole body of the Church is divided into the laity and the clergy, so the clergy are divided into presbyters and deacons.

I would prefer the term presbyter to that of priest; but it is not a matter of grave importance, although the word presbyter does actually seem more appropriate, and more in accord with the whole tenor of the Gospel of Jesus Christ.

The word presbyter is more appropriate than that of priest because it indicates spiritual fatherhood. It is the presbyters, chosen by God for their work, who spiritually beget us as sons through the spiritual birth of baptism. After we have become the sons of God through baptism, it is the presbyters who continue to care for us as fathers who have begotten us. Therefore, what better name could be given to these ministers of our new birth and continued nourishment than the reverend name of presbyters or fatherly guides? Throughout the body of the New Testament the Holy Ghost mentions presbyters frequently, but never calls them priests. I grant that the prophet Isaiah does say, "And I will also take of them for priests and for Levites, saith the Lord,"[1] but his use of the term, like that of the ancient Fathers, is only by way of analogy.

According to the true meaning of the New Testament, a presbyter is one "to whom our Savior Jesus Christ has given the power of spiritual procreation."[2] The whole population of Israel were the physical descendents of the twelve patriarchs.

[1] Is. 66. 21.
[2] Migne, S. G. xlii. 508.

THREE DEGREES OF ECCLESIASTICAL ORDER 117

Our Lord's Apostles we all acknowledge to be the patriarchs or progenitors of his whole Church, and so all the members of the Church are by the mystery of the heavenly birth the spiritual descendents of the twelve Apostles. St. John saw "upon the seats . . . four and twenty elders sitting;"[a] one half of these were the patriarchs of the Old Jerusalem, the other half were the Apostles of the New Jerusalem. The Apostles used this title for themselves, in spite of the fact that it was not an exclusive title for the apostolate, but was shared with the other presbyters.

The reason for this is that our Savior appointed some presbyters with greater power than others. Those who had the greater power had complete ministerial power, and those who had less power had incomplete ministerial power. It is true that the particular commission of the Apostles was the publication of the Gospel of Christ to all nations, and the delivery to them of the ordinances received by immediate revelation. This was their preeminence as Apostles; but besides this preeminence, their commission of office involved certain powers in addition to those of other presbyters. They were the powers of ordaining and consecrating other presbyters. The lesser presbyters could beget sons through baptizing, but could not create other presbyters.

The Apostles followed the example of Christ and not only created presbyters with full power, but ordained presbyters with lesser power. And that is just what our Savior had done as their example; for he not only commissioned Apostles, but he chose seventy other disciples whom he also made presbyters, but presbyters of less power than the Apostles, for they could preach and baptize but could not ordain and consecrate.

When the Apostles preached their first public sermon and four thousand souls were converted, more people were added to the number every day. When we remember that the Apostles

[a] Rev. 4. 4.

could not perform their ministerial duties in a public place, do we think it was possible that twelve men could have taught and administered the sacraments to such a great number of people in a great number of houses? Our Savior no doubt foresaw this harvest, and accordingly prepared laborers beforehand, so that, even though the Church grew so fast and so suddenly, there were enough presbyters on hand to take care of the situation. That is the reason that history does not tell us when presbyters were ordained in Jerusalem. They were already commissioned by Christ for their work, and we only read of the things which they did, and how presbyters were later made elsewhere.

To the two degrees of the ministry instituted by our Lord and Savior Christ, deacons were soon added by the appointment of Christ's Apostles. "Deacons, therefore, must know," says Cyprian, "that our Lord himself appointed Apostles, but that the Apostles ordained deacons after Christ's ascension into heaven."[1] Deacons were stewards in the Church, who were commissioned to distribute the goods of the Church, to provide goods for the poor, and to see that all financial matters were transacted religiously and faithfully. It was also their duty to serve the presbyters at the time of the divine service. Ignatius tells us of the dignity of the vocation of deacons, and says that their service to the bishop is like that of angelic powers.

These were the only duties of the deacons at the beginning. However, if the Church has, since that time, extended their ministry beyond the original limits of their labor, we must not think that the laws of the Scriptures have been violated, unless there is some prohibition in Scripture which has forbidden the Church that liberty. I note this particularly in regard to the licencing of deacons to preach, a kind of work that is different from that of the original diaconate, whose institution was at first for another purpose, namely, that of handling financial matters and serving the presbyters at the divine service.

[1] Migne., S. L. iv. 396.

THREE DEGREES OF ECCLESIASTICAL ORDER 119

The number of Christians increased in Jerusalem and became great. Then it became too much of a task for the Apostles both to teach and to minister to tables; and as they did not want to give up teaching, they appointed others to minister to the tables. The principle involved in this decision is the basis of an axiom which says that when the various phases of a man's work become so extensive that he can no longer manage it, the most natural way of solving the problem is to divide his work into parts and to surrender part of it to inferiors. This is the principle used by our Savior, for he placed the seventy presbyters under the twelve Apostles. Then the Apostles followed his example and placed seven deacons under both the twelve Apostles and the seventy presbyters.

If dividing duties is permissible, adding new duties should also be allowed. It seems reasonable that if deacons can handle their present duties, and can also do more, they ought to be allowed to undertake certain duties that belong to presbyters. Therefore, they ought to be allowed to preach. Just as there was a division of the presbyterate to form the diaconate, so a combination of certain of the functions of the presbyterate with those of the diaconate should be allowed.

It was an ancient custom of the Church to help the poor, especially widows. However, poor people are always querulous, and are inclined to think that they receive less than they should. Even when the Apostles did what they could without injury to their more important business, there were still some of the poor people who thought that others got too much and that they got too little. The Greek widows thought they got less food than the Hebrew widows. The Apostles then thought it was appropriate to ordain deacons to take care of these matters. The passage of time has destroyed the circumstances which originally made the diaconate necessary, and so deacons are now better employed in other duties; but even so, it still remains one of the degrees of order in the clergy of God, a degree of ministerial order instituted by the Apostles of Christ.

Epiphanius holds that the first seven deacons were chosen out of the number of the seventy disciples. This is an error, for it has never been considered appropriate to take men from higher occupations and place them in lower occupations. The Apostles wanted more freedom for teaching, and so they gave over the ministry of the tables to the deacons. Would it seem wise to take seven men from the seventy presbyters to make them ministers of the tables when Christ himself had commissioned them to be teachers?

We now see, therefore, for how long a time these three degrees of ecclesiastical order have existed in the Church of Christ. The highest and fullest in power is that of the Apostles; that which is next to it is the order of presbyters; and the lowest is the order of deacons.

CHAPTER XXI

Bishops in the Church of Christ

THE first bishops in the Church of Christ were his blessed Apostles. We know this because the office to which Matthias was chosen in succession to the place vacated by Judas was termed by the sacred history "episkope",[1] an episcopal office. This office is ascribed to Matthias, but it is as appropriate for all the Apostles as for him. That is the reason that St. Cyprian calls all of the Apostles bishops. They were called Apostles because Christ sent them out into the world to proclaim his Gospel; and they were also called bishops because he gave them the care of government. And the Apostles carried out their offices of episcopal authority quite as much by governing as they carried out their apostolical offices by teaching.

I grant that, though the word "episkope" does indicate that aspect of the office of Apostles which deals with government, it does not prove that they were the superior rulers. The term "episkope" was shared by them with their inferiors, and was not a term peculiar to the Apostles. The history of their actions, however, plainly indicates what meaning the name should bear, for the holy Apostles of Christ exercised such spiritual leadership as properly belongs to bishops. Therefore, they were bishops at large.

In due process of time the Apostles transmitted their episcopal authority to others, and gave it to them as a perpetual possession. "We are able to enumerate all of those," says Irenaeus, "who were made bishops by the Apostles."[2] He says that the Apostles made Linus the first bishop of Rome. Polycarp also tells us that the Apostles made him bishop of the Church of Smyrna. Ignatius tells us that the Apostles made Evodius

[1] Acts I. 20.
[2] Iren., lib. iii. c. 3.

bishop of Antioch. He tells us that when he exhorts that church to walk in the holy steps of their first bishop, and to follow his virtuous example.

The Apostles, therefore, were the first to have such authority, and all others have had it who have followed after them as their lawful successors. That is true where the later bishops are in the succession of a church in which an Apostle had jurisdiction, as in the case where Simon succeeded James in Jerusalem. It is also true where there has been a true succession of episcopal power although no Apostle was ever in charge of that particular church, for to be in the succession of the Apostles means to follow after them in the succession of power which was first given to them.

"All bishops," said Jerome, "are the successors of the Apostles."[3] Cyprian says something of the same sort, for he says that bishops are "overseers who succeed the Apostles through a vicarious ordination."[4] It seems to follow from all of this that those whom we now call bishops were at first usually called Apostles, and that is the reason the bishops even took the name of those very Apostles to whose offices of spiritual authority they succeeded.

Some people deny that the Apostles had any successors at all to their office of apostleship. This view need not contradict ours, if apostleship is properly understood. In some ways every presbyter is a successor of the Apostles; in other ways, only bishops are their successors; in still other ways the Apostles have no successors at all.

The Apostles were especially chosen eye-witnesses of Jesus Christ, and they had their ambassadorial commission directly from him. They were commissioned as the principal first founders of that Church of God made up of Gentiles as well as Jews. In all of these things they were unique, and none of their successors were like them. Yet the Apostles do at the

[3] Hieron., ep. 85.
[4] Cypr., *ep ad Flor.*

present time have their true successors on earth. Even though their successors' functions are not so wide as those of the Apostles, yet it is a succession to that kind of episcopal function which involves the power to sit as spiritual judges over both the laity and the clergy wherever the Christian churches are established.

St. Augustine says that "a bishop is superior to a presbyter;"[5] and now we have to determine in what respect the bishop is superior. His preeminence consists in two things: first, in the degree of power in his rank of ministerial order, and second, in the kind of power that involves jurisdiction. According to the Mosaic law, the priests had more power and authority than the Levites, and the high priests had greater authority than the lower priests. Therefore, the Levites were subordinate to the priests, and the lower priests to the high priests. The reason for this was that there were degrees of dignity and worth in the functions which they exercised, and not only because one had the power to command and control the other.

Similarly, the presbyter is more important and more worthy in office than the deacon. For that reason, the deacon is inferior to the presbyter. We say also that a bishop is always considered a presbyter's superior, even in the matter of ministerial functions. Therefore, we must necessarily assert the nature of the principle duties which a bishop has and a presbyter does not.

It has always been considered the peculiar power of the bishop to ordain both deacons and presbyters. This power is the power of giving orders to others, and belongs distinctly to bishops because it has never been considered right for the inferior presbyters to ordain. Ordination has great force and dignity, and is a power that belongs only to bishops. Presbyters have received the power to administer the sacraments, and are able to bear children to God; but bishops have the power of ordaining, and

[5] Aug., *ep 19*.

can create fathers to beget children for God. This is Epiphanius' appropriate way of describing the power of the presbyter and of the bishop.

There are some who say that there is no difference between a bishop and an inferior presbyter in the power of orders. The reason for this opinion is that presbyters as well as bishops are authorized to read prayers in the church, to preach the Gospel, to baptize, and to administer the holy eucharist. However, those who hold this have not considered the fact that the presbyter's authority to do these things is derived from the bishop who ordained him. Thus, even in the functions that are common to both the presbyter and the bishop the power of the presbyter is like a light borrowed from a lamp.

Ignatius tells us that there are two functions in the office of a bishop, those of priestly ministration and of ruling. The priestly functions of the bishop are of such preeminence that it is he only who has the heavenly mysteries of God commissioned to him. Therefore, except through ordination from him, and authority received from him, others are not permitted to be the ordinary ministers of God's Church. The other power of the sacred function of the bishop is the power of jurisdiction, and all of us know that the first Apostles themselves had jurisdiction, and, secondly, we know how Titus and Timothy had jurisdiction over presbyters. We also know that Christian bishops since that time have had a similar power.

When Ignatius compared bishops with deacons and with those ministers of the Word and sacraments who were only presbyters, he said, "What is the bishop but one who has all rule and power in so far as a man may have it, for in his power he is a follower of even God's own Christ."[6]

---

[6] Ignat., *ep. ad Smyr.*

PART FOUR

CHURCH AND STATE

CHAPTER XXII. Church and State as One
CHAPTER XXIII. The King as a Limited Sovereign
CHAPTER XXIV. The King as Temporal Head of the Church
CHAPTER XXV.   Christ as Supreme Sovereign
CHAPTER XXVI. Christ as Spiritual Head of the Church

CHAPTER XXII

Church and State as One

A church is naturally different from a commonwealth, because a commonwealth is defined in one way and a church in another way. There are people who hold that the Church and the commonwealth are corporations which are distinct not only in nature and definition but also in substance. According to their theory the members of the Church cannot perform any of the duties of the state, and the members of the state cannot perform any of the duties of the Church. If they do so, they violate the law of God, who divided them and requires that Church and state should function as independent entities because they are so completely separated. Each of them depends upon God, but neither depends upon the other's approval for anything it has to do.

Our opinion is the opposite of this, for we say that the care of religion should be the common concern of every state. Those states which embrace the true religion have the name of the Church in distinction from those states which do not accept the true religion. Every state, therefore, has a religion, but every state does not have the true religion; and only those states which have the true religion have the Church. It is the truth of religion that distinguishes a church from states which do not have the Church.

When we speak of true religion we are using the term in the broad sense, and not in the sense of every detail of religious truth. There are states which deviate from the truth in particular points, but which, in comparison with states which hold a heathen religion, may be said to profess the true religion. Thus, although in antiquity there were many states throughout the world, it was only the commonwealth of Israel which had the true religion and was for that reason the Church of God. The Church of Jesus Christ is made up of all the states which hold the religious truth that is distinctive of Christianity. Therefore, we may say that, as a state, a commonwealth maintains religion, and as a Church that state maintains that religion which God has revealed by Jesus Christ.

We see, therefore, that according to our view the Church is a society of men organized first of all as a public or civil government, and second distinguished from other states by the exercise of the Christian religion. With those, however, who take the opposite view from ours, the Church is a group of men united together and distinguished from other groups by the exercise of the Christian religion, and necessarily and perpetually divided from the body of the commonwealth. Even if we have a state made up exclusively of Christians, the Church of Christ and the commonwealth are two corporations each existing independently of each other.

Our view is different from that which holds that Church and state are two corporations. Here in England there is not a man who is a member of the Church of England who is not a member of the commonwealth; and there is not a man who is a member of the commonwealth who is not a member of the Church of England. The relation of Church and state is like the relation of the two sides and base of a triangle. The same line can be both a base and a side. It is a base if it happens to be the bottom and subtends the angle bounded by the two sides. If, on the other hand, one of the two sides is made a base, then the line that was previously a base becomes a side. This is a symbol of the relation of Church and state. A group of people is called a commonwealth in a certain relation, and the same group is called a Church in another relation. There is a distinction between Church and state, and yet the same group is both Church and state. Thus it is that no one who is a member of one can be denied to be a member of the other.

Those who disagree with us have a difficult position to maintain. To make their inferences valid they must hold that the Church and state are two distinct and separate societies, and that the members of one cannot belong to the other. As a matter of fact, they do not make such a radical separation, and thus their basis for their inferences is defective. Even so, they assert,—although without logical foundation,—that bishops may not meddle with affairs of the commonwealth because they are governors of another corporation which is the Church, and that kings may not make laws for the Church because they are rulers of another corporation which is the commonwealth.

Therefore, the walls of separation between Church and state must be maintained forever. They hold the necessity of Church and state as separate corporations, and that makes it absolutely impossible for one man to have the power of government in both. We hold a theory more consistent with the facts of the case, for we recognize that as the persons in both Church and state are the same, there is nothing to prevent the same person from ruling both.

The Church and the commonwealth, therefore, are a single corporation, which is called a commonwealth in relation to its secular law and government, and is called a church in relation to its submission to the spiritual law of Jesus Christ. These two sets of laws make necessary two different sets of offices, and therefore there are officers in charge of one set of laws and not the other; yet, society as a whole is not divided, and is not cut into two separate societies.

It will be said in opposition to our theory that the Fathers of the Church often speak of the state and the Church of God as in opposition. We know, say our opponents, that the same thing cannot be both itself and another. If the same society is both Church and state, how can one of the Fathers speak of Church and state flourishing together? What is meant when a Father speaks of one thing as the Church and another as the state? Finally, what is meant when one of the Fathers contrasts the affairs of the province with those of the Church? Is it not clear, they say, that Church and state are different corporations?

No, it is not clear that Church and state are always different corporations. We may speak of them as two; we may separate the rights and causes of one from the other in those respects in which there is a difference between them. However, there is no corporate difference. The truth is that Church and commonwealth are in one sense really different, but their difference lies in the attributes, and such attributes may and should exist harmoniously together in one subject. Therefore, the difference between these attributes does not prove that they inhere in different subjects. Although the subjects in which they inhere are different, as when the people of God live among infidels, the nature of the attributes is such that their subjects may be one. Therefore, it is not essential that the subjects in which these attributes inhere be diverse.

There cannot possibly be any mistake in our theory about this matter if we remember what that attribute is that makes a society into a commonwealth, and what the attribute is that makes a society into a church. A society is a commonwealth because it has a government or constitution under which its citizens live, and a society is a church because of the truth of the religion which that society professes.

A name of an attribute which is unabstracted from the subject in which it exists, indicates not only the attribute itself, but the subject in which the attribute inheres. When we describe a man as a schoolmaster or a physician, these names indicate not only two attributes, teaching and healing, but also a person or persons in whom the attributes inhere. In fact, there is nothing to prevent one man being both schoolmaster and physician, although the same man is usually not both at the same time.

The same is true of the use of the terms commonwealth and Church. These terms indicate not only the attributes, civil government and the Christian religion, but also the groups of people which are the subjects of these attributes. Their nature also is such that the two attributes may both inhere in the same subject. Although the attributes are themselves different, they do no always imply different subjects.

When, therefore, we contrast the Church with the commonwealth in Christian society, we mean by the commonwealth that society in relation to all its public affairs, except true religion, and we mean by the Church that same society in relation to true religion without reference to anything else. When that society which is both Church and state flourishes as a commonwealth, we say "the commonwealth flourishes." When that same society flourishes as a church we say "the Church flourishes." When that same society flourishes as a commonwealth and as a church, we say "the Church and the commonwealth flourish together."

CHAPTER XXIII

THE KING AS A LIMITED SOVEREIGN

THE general tenor of the argument that Church and state should always be separate indicates that in a Christian kingdom the one who has supreme power in a commonwealth may not lawfully have sovereign power over the Church. That means that he may not dispose and order spiritual affairs as the highest uncommanded commander of the Church. Those who hold this position have proposed the question whether the ecclesiastical power of the king as sovereign governor may be exercised lawfully by him as head and governor of the Church. To resolve this problem we must define what the power of sovereignty is, and then determine whether Christian kings may have it. In this chapter we will determine the nature of sovereignty, in the next whether the king may exercise it over the Church.

No one could live in a society that had no order, because if there were no order there would be utter confusion. If there were no order there would be no cohesion, and instead there would be division, and out of division inevitably there would be destruction. "Every kingdom divided against itself is brought to desolation; and a house divided against a house falleth."[1] The Apostle Paul, therefore, in giving advice to organized groups, said, "Let all things be done decently and in order."[2]

There can be no order in society unless the persons in that society know their place and duties within it. If there is an order among persons in society that means that they are distinguished by grades in society, for order is a matter of levels or grades. The whole world consists of many parts, and many

[1] Lk. 11. 17.
[2] 1 Cor. 14. 40.

different parts, and they are only sustained by order; the Creator of the world has set them in order. In fact, God himself has set down as a fundamental law that, wherever there is a joining together of many persons or things, the lowest should be united to the highest by their cohesion with that which is intermediary and is closest to them. Thus, unity of the whole is produced.

The order of things and persons in states is the work of polity, and the proper instrument of all forms of polity is power. Power is the capacity to act that we either have or receive from others. If the action is a matter of mere religion, the power to carry it out is spiritual; if this power has nothing superior in its domain to it, we call it sovereignty or supreme power in that country and domain.

It seems to me that there is no doubt that every independent group, before it has established any form of government, has under God's supreme authority full sovereignty over itself. In the same way, a man who is not subject to someone else has a like supreme power over himself. When God created man he gave him full power to govern himself and to choose the kind of society in which he would live. A man who is born his own master may become another's servant; a whole society which naturally has the power over itself may hand that power to one man, to a few men, to many men, and then the rest of that society will live in subjection to those who rule.

Some groups are brought into subjection by force. When they are subdued in this way they must submit to whatever type of yoke it pleases their conquerors to lay upon them. Sometimes it pleases God by special appointment to choose and nominate the ones to whom sovereignty shall be given. That was true of the commonwealth of Israel. Sometimes the supreme power is given according to human discretion when God leaves a group free to make their own choice of a governor.

It makes no difference by whatever means kings or governors

obtain their position, we must admit that their lawful choice is approved by God, and that they are themselves God's lieutenants and we must confess that their power is his.

The word of God does not give the supreme power to all kings in ecclesiastical affairs, neither does it say that any king should not have it. Therefore, it is wholly a matter of human right that kings are given such sovereignty. However, even if the power of government is bestowed by human choice, those who hold it, hold it by divine right. In his revealed word, God has granted such powers to rulers although he does not himself directly appoint them, but leaves the appointment to human beings. Even though the appointment is human, there is no doubt that the duties we owe to those who govern are prescribed by the word of God, and consequently are required by every right.

Let us take an example. The power which the Roman emperors had over foreign provinces was not instituted by the law of God, neither was Tiberius Caesar invested with his commission from heaven. Even so, the payment of tribute to Caesar as emperor was the plain law of Jesus Christ. Kings are kings by human right, but they are due honor by divine right. Human laws are presupposed as obligatory by the statutes of God. That is the reason that the law of God commands us to acknowledge as God's lieutenants those men who have their positions lawfully as governors, and to confess that their power is his. However, the rulers are also required by the same law of God to use their power in so far as they can to do God honor.

The law does not appoint any man as a given woman's husband; but if a woman marries a man, the law of God gives him authority over her. The law of God does not command us to have monarchies in the Christian world; but if we do have such a government the law gives the king the right to require general obedience of his subjects in whatever matters his royal power gives him the right to command. Human beings may give authority to kings, and if they do so, the law of God requires that the men who have given such authority to the king should obey him as their ruler.

All kings do not have the same degrees of sovereignty. Kings who are kings by conquest dictate their own terms. For that reason we cannot certainly define how great their power is, either civil or spiritual, except to say that they are governed by the general law of God and of nature. Kings whom God has appointed have that degree of power which God has assigned and approved.

The kings who were instituted by human agreement have the extent of their power indicated by the articles of compact between them and their people. They are bound not only by the articles of contract when the crown was first established, for those articles are now unknown or else known by very few, but they are also bound by more recent agreements with their people. These more recent agreements are revealed in positive laws or immemorial customs enshrined in the common law. And so by means of such agreements even the thrones originally established by conquest have gradually come to be that most pleasing form of royal government, of which Aristotle says, "The kingship . . . was based on general consent but limited to a number of definite functions, with the king acting as general and judge and head of religious observances."[3]

I am not of the opinion that the best form of government is that in which the king's power is the most absolute, but rather the form in which the power is limited in the best possible way. The most limited form of royal sovereignty is that in which the king can deal with the fewest possible things. That, I do not think, is the best form, but rather the best form of royal sovereignty is that which is legally bound by the soundest, most perfect, and most impartial rule. That rule is the law, and I mean by law not only the law of nature and

---

[3]Arist., *Pol.*, 1285 b 22f. (Barker's translation).

the law of God, but all national and municipal law which is agreeable to the law of nature and the law of God.

That people whose law in ultimate matters is their king is happier than a people whose king is their law. Where the king guides the state and the law guides the king, that state is like a harp or a harmonious instrument whose strings are played by a single musician, but played according to the rules and laws of musical harmony. It is for this reason that I cannot choose but commend most highly the men who laid the foundations of this commonwealth. In it every person is subject to the royal power, yet that royal power is limited and must proceed according to the law. The axioms of our royal government are, (1) the law makes the king, and (2) the king can do nothing unless he does it according to the law.

When our kings, therefore, take over authority, the very rites of their inauguration indicate before their eyes how far by law their sovereign power and authority extend. They are crowned, they are enthroned, they are anointed. The crown is the symbol of their military power, the throne is the symbol of their judicial power, the oil is the symbol of their religious power.

CHAPTER XXIV

THE KING AS TEMPORAL HEAD OF THE CHURCH

IT is a flagrant error to think that the royal power should be used for the good of the body and not of the soul, and for men's temporal peace and not for their eternal salvation. If this is so conceived, it is to think that God has appointed kings for no other purpose except to fatten up people like hogs and to see that they have their mast to eat. Of course, we admit that kings do not lead men to salvation by means of secret, invisible, and spiritual rule, or by the outward administration of things that belong to the priestly order, such as the word and the sacraments.

However, because kings cannot exercise the functions of the ministry, that does not prove that they are incapable of supreme authority in external government, and are incapable of handling the affairs of religion in so far as they are subject to human authority. There is no reason to think that kings are incapable of such rule because religion is everlastingly beneficial to those who faithfully follow it.

The Jewish Church was administered in its temporal aspects by the king, and if it was allowed in their case, there is little reason why it should not be exercised by Christian kings. There is no reason why Christian kings should not exercise such power because the dignity and perfection of our religion is more than the Jewish.

It may be said, however, that the affairs of Christianity require more intelligence, more study, more knowledge of divine matters in the ruler than the Jewish religion did, and therefore a Christian king cannot exercise the authority over religion which a Jewish king did. We do not deny that the form of external government and the rites and ceremonies were laid down for the Jewish king in more detail than they are for the Christian ruler. That made it easier for the Jewish king. However, we must remember that the very detail of the Jewish law made the burden of ecclesiastical rule much more difficult for the Jewish than for the Christian king. There were innumerable doubts and difficulties produced by the very obscurity of their law, and if these doubts were not first resolved, the law could not possibly be enforced.

As the Jewish law also dealt with all kinds of civil affairs, their clergy, as interpreters of the whole law, had not only the work that our divines have to do, but also that of our lawyers. Therefore, the task of the Christian king is more difficult than the Jewish, and we must grant that in Christian states there must be a decision made about religious matters that requires more wisdom than most kings have. Nevertheless, their lack of expert ability does not prevent them from having the same royal authority which the kings of Israel had in those affairs of religion. Christian kings have the same sovereignty as the kings of Israel, and that sovereignty allows them to rule and command as supreme governors.

If we consider the Jewish economy, it will be easier to judge whether our kings exercise a legitimate sovereignty over the Church or not. There are people who think that the kings of England should not be called heads of the Church. We mean by head that the king has supreme power in ecclesiastical matters. If the king is head of the Church by law, why do they want to make it unlawful for us to call him by that name? If supreme power is permitted, why is the title head condemned? It is generally admitted that the sovereignty of the king is supreme over both persons and things. When we say that the king is the head of the Church we are only saying that he has the supreme government, not only of other things but of the Church as well.

When we say this, perhaps someone will reply that it is not

merely a matter of words but of facts; for however we interpret our words, it is not proper for any mortal man,—and that includes the civil magistrate,—to be treated as the head of the Church. Was not Christ, says our opponent, given the title head of the Church because he was "far above all principality, and power, and might, and dominion, and every name that is named, not only in this world, but also in that which is to come"?[1] If we use this name also for the civil magistrate, says our opponent, then it is clear that there is a power on earth who is the equal of Jesus Christ.

However, the king's office and sovereignty which we indicate by the title head of the Church, differs in three ways from the headship of Christ: it differs in order, in amount, and in kind. First, Christ's headship differs from the king's in order because God has made Christ head of the Church, "far above all principality, and power, and might, and dominion, and every name that is named, not only in this world, but also in that which is to come."[2] The power of all other rulers is, however, subordinate to his rule.

Second, the rule of the king as head of the Church differs from the headship of Christ in the amount of power involved. God has given Christ "the uttermost parts of the earth" for his "possession".[3] God has given him sovereignty over all places, persons, and things, a sovereignty that belongs to him exclusively and is not passed on in any succession, because Christ rules as head and king forever.

Christ is not bound by any kind of law except that of his own will and wisdom. His power is absolute, and is the same for his universal sway as it is for his sway over each province. Such absolute and universal rule belongs to no other ruler, for the king's rule is limited as we have seen. So when we say of Christ that he is head of the Church we mean that he has such

[1] Eph. 1. 21.
[2] Ibid.
[3] Ps. 2. 8.

absolute power that neither man nor angel may be compared with him.

The third, and most important, difference between Christ and the king is a difference in the kind of power they have. The head is the most excellent part of a man's body, and rules the rest. It has sensation and motion; and is the throne from which the soul reigns. It is the court from which all directions of the man's life proceed. The very character of the head, as the most excellent part of the body, as the throne of the soul, and as the court of all human affairs, indicates why Christ is called head of the Church. The head is the highest part of man, and there is nothing above it. The head is always united with the body. Thus, Christ too is the highest being in his Church and is inseparably united with it.

The head furnishes insight and movement to the whole body. Christ gives life to the whole body, he gives the whole body an understanding of heavenly things and strength to walk in the light of this understanding. Christ is not sensibly present on earth, and he is not visibly joined to his body here on earth, and that is because his corporal presence is in heaven. Christ does not administer the external rule of the external actions of the Church, but by the secret inward influence of his grace gives spiritual life and the strength of spiritual motion to it. Therefore, it is quite obvious that there is a difference of operation between his headship and that of kings.

The king exercises an altogether visible headship, and only orders the external structure of the Church's affairs in its temporal order. The king's headship is obviously different from Christ's, even in its very nature and kind. Christ's headship is unique, he is united with the Church in a unique way; he works in a unique way; and his uniqueness in union with the Church and in his work either in relation to the whole Church, a particular church, or any individual man, is like no other besides himself.

CHAPTER XXV

Christ as Supreme Sovereign

THE sovereignty and the headship of the king are, both in nature and in kind, obviously different from those of Christ, for Christ's rule is unique and he is exalted as head above all. In this chapter we will make clear the character of his sovereignty, and in the next his headship over the Church.

The sovereignty of Christ is related to that of God, the Father. Each day, when we pray the Lord's Prayer, we acknowledge that to God belongs "the kingdom, and the power, and the glory, forever."[1] We admit that God is "the King eternal, immortal, invisible, the only wise God," to whom belong "honour and glory for ever and ever."[2] What the Father does as Lord and King he does not do without the Son but by means of the Son. The Son, by his coeternal generation from the Father, receives from the Father the power which the Father possesses as his own. That is the reason our Savior says about his own rule, "All power is given unto me in heaven and in earth."[3] The Father created the world by the Son, and now guides it all by the Son. Therefore, Christ has supreme sovereignty over the whole world.

Christ is God. Christ is Logos, or the consubstantial Word of God. Christ is also that consubstantial Word who was made man. Christ as God said of himself, "I am Alpha and Omega, the beginning and the ending . . . which is, and which was, and which is to come, the Almighty."[4] As the consubstantial Word of God, he had with God before the beginning of the

---
[1] Mat. 6. 13.
[2] 1 Tim. 1. 17.
[3] Mat. 28. 18.
[4] Rev. 1. 8.

world, that glory which he requested that he might have as man. "And now, O Father, glorify thou me with thine own self with the glory which I had with thee before the world was."[5] For it is not necessary that everything said about Christ should be asserted of his Deity alone, or of his humanity alone; some things are asserted of him as the consubstantial Word of God, and some things are asserted of him as the Word incarnate.

At the beginning, the supreme power of government was exercised by the Son of God; but now it is most appropriately in the hands of the Son of Man. The Word made flesh, who is enthroned forever as King, reigns as sovereign Lord over all. The highest powers of government belong to the royal office of Christ, just as propitiation and mediation belong to his priestly office, and instruction to his prophetic office. His rule is of diverse kinds, and depends upon the state of those who are subject to it. He now rules the world, and some day will come again to judge the whole world. His rule is absolute, and therefore his royal power cannot be restricted to a mere portion of the world.

Despite his absolute sovereignty, some men do not show dutiful submission to him, and the obedience which they owe to him. Therefore, over those who do admit his sovereignty, he is said to be Lord *par excellence,* just as according to the Apostle Paul, God "is the Saviour of all men, especially of those that believe."[6] Those who come to believe and obey him are always spoken of as men who have attained the citizenship of the Kingdom; for those who are in the Kingdom, Christ is "the author of eternal salvation."[7]

The citizens of the Kingdom have a high kind of spiritual fellowship with God, with Christ, and the saints, for as St. John says, "Our fellowship is with the Father," and not only with

[5] Jn. 17. 5.
[6] 1 Tim. 4. 10.
[7] Heb. 5. 9.

the Father, but, he adds, "with his Son, Jesus Christ,"[8] and with the saints. The Apostle Paul expresses it somewhat more fully, "But ye are come unto Mt. Sion, and unto the city of the living God, the heavenly Jerusalem, and to an innumerable company of angels, to the general assembly and church of the firstborn, which are written in heaven, and to God the Judge of all, and to the spirits of just men made perfect, and to Jesus the mediator of the new covenant."[9] That means the citizens of the Kingdom are members of that mystical body which we call the Church of Christ. As for those who are outside of the Kingdom, they are aliens from the commonwealth of Israel, and they are in the kingdom of darkness because they exist in this present world without God. Our Savior's lordship over these aliens is therefore a sovereignty over rebels; but his lordship over those who obey him is a sovereignty over dutiful subjects.

Christ's providential rule preserves mankind by sustaining kingdoms, and not only those which are obedient to him but also those which rebel against him. Therefore, all kingdoms are sustained by the divine power. He not only sustains kingdoms, but he sustains and preserves his Church, for his providence works for the safety of God's elect. Christ gathers together the elect of God. He inspires them, comforts them, and preserves his Church in every possible way.

He not only preserves the state, he also preserves the Church. Christ as God has provided certain means for gathering together and keeping those who constitute the Church. This is the way in which he governs his Church; and in this government he has none above him, just as he has none above him in the government of commonwealths.

Christ says, "Where two or three are gathered together in my name, there am I in the midst of them."[10] He also says that he will be with them, till the world's end. These promises

[8] 1 Jn. 1. 3.
[9] Heb. 12. 22-24.
[10] Mat. 18. 20.

he makes as the Lord and governor of the Church, and that means that he has no superior in the Church.

His rule over the Church militant must necessarily cease when the Church militant ceases in the world. Generals of armies surrender their commissions when they have finished their work, for they give up the commissions that were given them for a certain purpose when that purpose is achieved. Then they no longer have their former authority, but are in the state of inferiors rather than superiors.

So it will be with Jesus Christ, for when the end of all things comes, the Son of Man will do the same thing as these generals. Although he will have reigned until the end of the world, he will then surrender his government of the Church militant on earth. When the warfare on earth is over, he will surrender his lordship and his sovereignty over his brethren as their king and general in the battles of this earth. Then there will be no difference between them and him in sovereignty. They will no longer be warriors under his command, but they, together with him, will be under the kingship of God, and, together with Christ, will receive the joys of everlasting triumph.

Then God will be all in all, and the lot of the wicked will be misery because of God's justice, and the lot of the righteous will be joy and bliss because of his love. In the meantime, Christ rules over this world as King, and has no superior in his rule, whether it be a rule over kingdoms or over the Church.

In the Old Testament it is said of Christ, "By me kings reign, and princes decree justice. By me princes rule, and nobles, even all the judges of the earth."[11] In the New Testament we find the same thing, for it says of Christ that he is "the prince of the kings of the earth."[12] We must now make clear how all authority of man over man is derived from God

[11] Prov. 8. 15-16.
[12] Rev. 1. 5.

through Christ, and must therefore be acknowledged by Christian men as delegated by Christ and under his sovereignty. To explain this we must recognize that whatever has necessary being has its source in the Son of God. Those things have necessary being in the world, without which the world cannot continue to exist. Therefore, a matter of so great utility as human government and sovereignty in government must have their source in him and be subordinate to him.

If we consider the authority of civil governmental officers in ecclesiastical affairs, we realize that this authority is from God through Christ, as all other good things are. Therefore, it cannot be held except as authority received from Christ. There is a power that is used for regulating religion. This regulation and constitutional order must flow from his authority. It is an authority, however, that has its source in his special care for the guidance and government of his people. Therefore, this authority over the Church, exercised by civil authority, is an especial authority derived from him. It comes from him as head of the Church, and not from him as the general Lord over the world. As the Apostle Paul says when speaking to the Church, "All are yours; and ye are Christ's; and Christ is God's."[22]

Kings are under Christ's dominion as members of the Church, and kings are under Christ as kings. Kings are members of the Church because they are part of the Church. They are kings because they have authority over the Church. This does not mean that they collectively have a power over the Church, but each one has control over a part of the Church. That means that the king has power over each individual within that church which is located in the realm where he is king.

We cannot deny that the king's sovereignty extends both to each man's person and to every realm of life, and this is a lawful exercise of power. The sovereign power has a unique character, and is like no other power in the world, and because of the

[22] 1 Cor. 3. 22-23.

uniqueness of this power, the sovereigns of the state are called heads. They have authority from Christ because he is the Lord over all. The civil authorities receive their authority from Christ because all lawful powers come from him. Therefore, the civil magistrate has his power as head of Christ's people as an inferior head under Christ as the supreme head.

CHAPTER XXVI

Christ as Spiritual Head of the Church

BECAUSE human weakness makes it necessary to have many rulers where the burden is too much for one man, Jethro persuaded Moses to have a number of rulers, each to take care of part of the responsibility of government, which as a whole was too much for Moses by himself. That was because one man was not strong enough for the whole task, and several governors were necessary. Although there is no such defect or weakness in Christ, there are many more reasons than we can search into, why it is wise for him to divide his kingdom into many portions, and to place many heads over it. Thus, the limited power with which each individual ruler governs makes manifest the greatness of Christ's unlimited authority.

Christ is always spiritually united with every part of his body, the Church; but we all know that Christ's visible and corporal presence is as far removed from every church here on earth as heaven is from earth. Visible government is necessary for the Church, and it is not clear how the exercise of visible government over the great numbers of people who are scattered everywhere throughout the world is possible without many visible governors. Since these governors have the greatest power that is possible for earthly rulers to have, they are rightly called heads. It is true that our Savior is always spiritually united with the parts of his mystical body; but visible government by heads of states, endued with supreme power and having that power limited within a certain territory, is necessary for the exercise of visible government.

The body of Christ consists of the entire Church, and every member of the Church is a member of that body. However, the one who has supreme authority and power over all the rest is not an inferior member of the body. By making the magistrate the ruler of his own domain, we make him a member who is not subject to the rule of any other person within the visible Church. However, the magistrate has a place in the Church, and that place is that of the supreme ruler.

There are many heads of these visible bodies, but there is only one who is head of that spiritual body of which these visible rulers are only inferior members. As a matter of fact, these visible rulers may be outside of the spiritual body of Christ, but even so, we ought to honor them because they have the highest authority in the visible order. However, although the ruler is head of the church in his dominion, that does not prevent him from being a member of the Church of God.

The headship of Christ as universal head over kings as particular heads is no more superfluous than the presence of a supreme head over many inferior heads in any other organization. That is the way armies and civil corporations are organized, for the figure of a biological organism is not perfectly analogous to a body politic, since in the human or animal body more than one head is superfluous, but in the body politic several heads are not superfluous.

It is neither unnatural nor inappropriate for a church to have more than one head. If there are many Christian churches and every one of them is complete in itself, and Christ is Lord and head over them all, why do we think it is more unnatural for one body to have two heads than it is for one head to have so many bodies? God has made Christ the supreme head of the whole Church. He has made him head not only of the mystical body, which the eye of man cannot see, but he has made him head of every Christian state and every visible church in the world.

Let us make the whole matter of leadership as clear as possible. The government of the Church is a spiritual government of Christ, and is that government by which the Church is ruled and governed in spiritual matters. There are two distinct kinds of this spiritual government. One is a government exercised invisibly by Christ himself in his own Person. The other kind of government is an outward administration by persons who are permitted by Christ to rule over his Church.

Christ as spiritual and invisible ruler is in a unique sense the head of the Church of God. No other creature is head of the Church in the sense that Christ is, because that invisible lordship is the rule over our souls by the hand of the blessed Spirit, by which we are sealed and marked and made particularly his. Christ alone is the Lord who dwells, lives, and reigns in our hearts. He alone is the head who gives salvation and life to his body. He alone is the fountain from which the heavenly grace flows, and passes to every part, for his grace flows forth through the word, the sacraments, and discipline.

Moreover, the power of administering the word, the sacraments, and discipline of the Church of Christ is called the power of order, and is a spiritual power, and is Christ's power. It is spiritual because its duties properly concern the spirit, and because he instituted these duties. However, the ministerial exercise of these duties is not inward and spiritual but outward and visible, and hence is not spiritual because visible, and not his because it is not his act but the minister's.

The king's rule, like that of the clergy, belongs to the second kind of spiritual rule, which is external and visible, and yet is spiritual because of its matter, and Christ's because it is done with his approval. However, it must be distinguished from the kind of government which is his very own spiritual rule because he does not administer it in his own Person. We recognize this rule of the king as visible and external in the Church, and we recognize it as exercised by men, and we recognize it as distinct from the spiritual power of Christ's own government. Christ's own rule is spiritual because it works secretly, inwardly, and invisibly. It is called his because it is his own personal rule, and it is a rule by him and him alone. In this sense he is our head, yet, in regard to external and visible government, there are other heads besides him, and we can hold this without any contradiction at all.

Some of the ancient Fathers say that there is only one head of the Church, and he is Christ. They say that the minister who baptizes cannot be over the man who is baptized because Christ is head of the whole Church. Paul, therefore, could not be the head of the churches which he planted, because Christ is the head of the whole body. When they use language of this sort, they are speaking of Christ as head of the Church in that unique and inward sense in which he declared that he alone personally rules. In that sense no other is head, not even head of the smallest part of the whole Church. In this sense the one who baptizes, baptizes in the name of Christ; the one who converts, converts in the name of Christ; the one who rules, rules for Christ. The whole Church can have but one head who is Lord over all. Therefore, if Christ is this sort of head, no other can be lord either of the whole Church or of any part of it.

www.ingramcontent.com/pod-product-compliance
Lightning Source LLC
Chambersburg PA
CBHW071433160426
43195CB00013B/1889